# O u c h !

## Life Can Hurt, But Healing
## Is Your Choice

## Susan R. Germanson

*To Joan — I hope it
there is healing.
healing. Psalm 71:20
God Bless You
Susan*

**VANTAGE PRESS**
New York

*Cover art and drawings by Earl Keleny*
*© by Earl Keleny*
*ekeleny@aol.com*

A portion of the proceeds from this book will go to battered women's shelters.

Published by Vantage Press, Inc.
516 West 34th Street, New York, New York 10001

Manufactured in the United States of America
ISBN: 0-533-13481-1

Library of Congress Catalog Card No.: 99-97765

0 9 8 7 6 5 4 3 2 1

To my daughter, Ana Maria, who is an inspiration to me as she continues to courageously live life to the fullest.

# Contents

# Acknowledgments

I would like to thank God who has always been there for me, unconditionally, through the great and tough times. Next I want to thank my parents, Jerry and Ellie, for constantly believing in me, and for being such active/selfless parents. In addition, I am grateful to the rest of my family who have been a great support for me. A huge thank-you to Lisa, Jack, Walter and Paul for always standing by my side. I need to thank my shrink, Jim, for his incredible insight into my life and healing journey. A special thank-you goes to Sandy, my lifelong friend. Next, I am grateful to Peter, Jack, Shelle, and Ronda for helping me to pick up the pieces of my life. Thanks, Pearl, you are the greatest kindred spirit of all. Gary, thanks for your beautiful music that has been instrumental in my healing process. Thanks to Margarita, Vicky, Leslie, and Laura for your friendship. My greatest appreciation is to David and Earl for believing in me and this book. Finally, thanks to all of my athletes/students, who have been an absolute joy!

This book is written in memory of three students/athletes of mine—Becky Blake, Ricky Thomas, Jr., and Ian Scott.

# Author's Note

## How do I use this book?

I am in too much pain and I just can't bear to read <u>another book!</u>

## Please take a few moments to read this part!!!

1. If you are in the midst of searing pain or the onset of a tragedy, it is imperative that you read **Part 1 Surviving in a Crisis as soon as possible.** It is short, to the point and packed with the most important information that you need right now!! It is easy to read and should only take you about fifteen minutes. Many have wished that they would have known this back when the storms of life hit them.

2. There are special pages for you to write your own **personal notes and ideas** at the end of each chapter. This is **your** book. Take the ideas and adapt/tailor make them so that they work for you!!

3. **Get a highlighter/magic marker**, and highlight as you go along. You may need to read something over again, or refer back to some specific advice. You may be too depressed, or hurried to read the book over again. All you want to do is find that one part without a lot of hassle. Also feel free to write reminders in the margins. Then you will be able to find the certain part that you desperately need.

4. **<u>Feel free to jump around!</u>** You may not need to read this book from cover to cover. Parts of this book may not pertain to your situation! At some point in time, do read the book cover to cover, because it can help you to become more understanding and compassionate. You will develop your friendship skills, and be able counsel/help other people in crisis on a higher level.

5. Just start reading, take courage, dig down deep, and conquer your pain. Tragedy is a fight, better said, it is a battle! Many times it comes down to survival of the fittest. I give my best to you in your journey to wholeness.
   **YOU CAN DO IT!**

# Part 1
# Surviving in a Crisis

It is crucial for people to read this first part of the book immediately after the onset of a tragedy. It is easy to get wrapped up in the grief, denial, shock and to become so dysfunctional that we forget to take care of ourselves. These first five chapters provide simple advice about living moment by moment, taking care of ourselves, reaching out for help, acknowledging the pain, and focusing on healing.

# 1

# Your Only Goal: Live Moment by Moment

When you are in the midst of a crisis, your only goal should be to live moment by moment—not day by day, or hour by hour, but moment by moment. This single goal may sound trite and obvious, but truly grasping its meaning and putting it into action can be very challenging. If you are the kind of person who is used to planning ahead and getting things done, you must put all long-range goals on the shelf for some time. Put short-range goals there, too. When people go through a very stressful time, their coping skills and their decision-making skills are diminished. If performing ordinary everyday tasks is barely possible, looking ahead just one week can make everything seem impossible. If making any decision is difficult, this is not the time to make big decisions. Concentrate on the present. Concentrate on living from one moment to the next. This is the first step to getting better.

When Sara's counselor advised her that her only goal should be to make it through each day one day at a time, she thought, *"What stupid advice, of course I can make it through the day. What a piece of cake!"* However, after two days of trying to follow that advice, to wake up each day and do her best to just make it through the day, Sara was astonished by how difficult it was. Sometimes she wondered if she could meet the challenge of making it through just one hour! That is when Sara realized that before she could live one day at a time, she had to learn how to live moment by moment. So each day when she awakened, she would say,

*"All I need to do is make it through this day by learning to live moment by moment. I'll try to get done what I NEED to get done for just this day. I'll do my best to focus on what I am to do. I will be gentle to myself if I don't get some things done."*

At first you will SURVIVE moment by moment. Then, little by little, you will start to FUNCTION moment by moment. As you heal, you will begin to LIVE moment by moment. Hopefully, you will get to the point where you ENJOY life one moment at a time. As you progress from surviving to functioning to living, the moments will expand into hours, the hours stretch into days, and you will find you have moved past the point of just living so that you are actually enjoying life. We all need to stop trying to conquer the world and just live!

> Let me be willing to live this year in a way that will be gentle to myself . . . moment by moment.
> —The Author

***Personal notes and ideas***

What does "moment by moment" mean to me?

What must I do to actually live moment by moment?

# 2

# Take Care of Yourself

Let's face it, hardship and pain are a part of life. But being miserable is a choice! You can become *bitter* or you can become *better*. One of the first steps to becoming better is to take care of yourself.

## A. Eat Right

It is important that you EAT GOOD FOOD. Even if you don't feel like eating, take (or make) time to eat something—a piece of bread and butter, a cup of soup, or a glass of juice. Don't hurt your body by starving yourself or by overindulging in junk food. This can turn into a vicious circle.

If you stop eating, you are putting your body in danger. It is imperative that your body gets healthy nutritional food in order that you have the strength to make it through the day. It is nearly impossible to deal with your pain if your body is not properly fed.

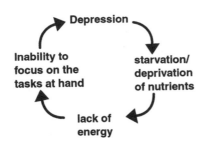

Some people tend to anesthetize their pain through food. They feel so out of control that they start overindulging and subsequently gain a lot of weight. This results in becoming more angry, frustrated, and miserable. Now a tough circle begins that is very hard to break/stop. Don't take a "who cares?" attitude with your body. Yes, part of your life has been turned upside down, but don't allow the eating issue to get the best of you. Fight back, break the cycle before it turns into a "snowball effect." It is amazing the influence that body weight has over one's emotions. The people who medicate on food to make themselves feel better need to find a healthier source of consolation. Gaining a lot of weight can have adverse effects on a person emotionally, physically, socially, spiritually, and occupationally.

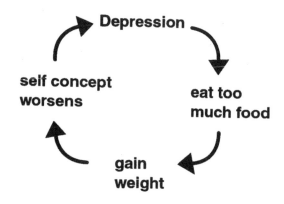

## B. Exercise

Don't be a couch potato! Too much television is a bad thing. Do something physically active! Even a short walk around the block can make you feel better. It is amazing what exercise and the outdoors can do for you. It won't cure your problems, but it will improve your overall health so that you can deal with your pain. Sometimes exercise is the last thing you want to do or feel you can do. If so, force yourself, but do it out of kindness to yourself. Exercise is beneficial, not only to your physical health, but also to your emotional health. You can safely vent a lot of anger through physical activity and sports. For example, find a backboard and hit tennis balls against it as hard as you can. If you are a swimmer, do flip turns and really work them hard. If you are not an athlete, a brisk walk or low impact aerobics can help.

## C. Treat yourself

The purpose of treating yourself is to reassure that you are taking care of yourself, to show that you love yourself. But don't overindulge. Many tragic situations are accompanied by financially tough times. You don't want to spend yourself into financial disaster while trying to make yourself feel better. There are also countless free or low cost ways to feel better. Buy a new CD, soak in a scented bath, treat yourself to an afternoon at a museum, check your newspaper for free civic or cultural events. . . . However, make sure you give yourself a small gift or treat every now and then. You deserve it!

## D. Laugh (Don't be a person who has a severe case of seriousness.)

Relearning to laugh is vital to getting better. Find some humor in each day. Schedule fun in your life daily. Watch your favorite TV sitcom. Go to a funny movie. Spend time with a hilarious friend. Keep a light-hearted book of cartoons next to your bed so you can close each day with a few chuckles and go to sleep without a heavy heart. Some nights even a funny book will be too hard to manage—and that is OK—but most of the time, those good old cartoons will give you the precious laughter that you need to help you cope.

Beware of movies filled with horror, tragedy, and violence. They are out of the question! So are a lot of television programs. What you need is humor and fun, not something that pulls you down deeper.

## E. Listen to Music

Music can soothe your soul and cheer you up. Listen to your favorite music as much as possible, even if that means listening to the same music tape or C.D. twice a day. Find music that has a calming effect on you. Light some candles, turn off the lights, wrap yourself up in a blanket, and let the music fill your soul. Make sure the music is inspirational, not depressing.

And don't forget about the benefits of upbeat, happy songs. Turn up the volume, and sing at the top of your lungs. For those who like dancing . . . it is a great way to forget about your problems, get some exercise, and just have fun.

## F. Keep in Touch with Friends

You are the one who knows when you need time alone and when you need company, so don't wait for other people to contact you. You need to take the initiative, especially on those days when you know you can't be alone. Your friends are there to help you when you need them, but you can't expect them to pamper you. They have their own lives and responsibilities. It's up to you to pick up the phone and connect with them.

## G. Return to "Normal" Living

As soon as possible, go back to whatever "normal" living has been for you—work, school, volunteerism. Getting back to what was your familiar routine will temporarily give you a break from all your stress.

Doing things that contribute to society and helping others in need not only can give your mind a break from your problems, but also can put your problems in a new perspective. After helping someone, you might discover that the sharp pain in your heart has temporarily turned into a dull ache. There is something soothing and satisfying in knowing that you have helped someone else.

## H. Be Spontaneous

Put some spice back into your life by trying something new or something you haven't done in a long time. Spontaneity is good for the soul, helps you get out of the doldrums, and doesn't have to cost a lot of money. Go for a bike ride along a special path. Take a scenic drive in the countryside. Invite a friend to your favorite coffee shop, or search out a new place for your coffee breaks. Visit a friend from the past. Take a trip far away. Ride the train instead of driving your car. Learn a new sport or take a dance class. The options are limitless! Be creative and go for it!

You can make it <u>work</u>
or
you can make it <u>worse.</u>

—The Author

*Personal notes and ideas*

How can I take care of myself?

How can I make it work?

How can I make it worse?

# 3

# Reach Out

No matter how much you admire self-sufficiency in others or strive for it yourself, this is not the time to do that. Do not even think about handling this by yourself! Confide in a couple of trustworthy friends or family members. Let them know you need their help, and ask them to check up on you often, perhaps daily. As time goes on, their calls won't need to be so frequent.

# A. Decision Making

You may not be very RATIONAL right now. This can happen when people go through a stressful time. Often their coping skills are diminished, making it hard to think clearly. Confer with your confidants before making any big decisions that you may regret later.

# B. Find a Support Group

A group of people who are experiencing or have dealt with the same difficulties as you can help immensely. These people can let you know that you aren't alone, that the pain will eventually go away, that if they survived the challenge, then so can you! So to find the right support group for you, ask friends, check the yellow pages, call a church, hospital, mental health center, or community educational program.

# C. Talk with a Professional

Find a good "shrink"/counselor/therapist. Family and friends are important, but trained professionals have more to offer in other ways. They can be objective because they don't have emotional ties to you. They can offer sound advice based on their years of training and practice.

If you are hesitant to seek professional help, remember that people who do seek such help are courageous and really being honest with themselves. Admitting the need for help is healthier than pretending you have it "all together."

Don't be reluctant to change counselors if you are uncomfortable with the first one you see. Give the therapist a chance, and then look for another if need be. You must be comfortable if you are going to make progress.

## D. Seek Spiritual Guidance

Confide in your spiritual leader. He or she may be able to help you cope with your grief process, to present a different perspective about your situation, to act as a guide when you explore answers to the many questions raised by your troubles. If you have never considered tapping into your faith, maybe now is a good time to do so. It is never too late! People who have chosen to explore their spiritual self later on in life have been very glad they did. They often wish that they would have done it earlier.

## E. Find Fun Friends

Give yourself a break from your sorrow by spending time with "fun friends." Choose people who are especially good at distracting you from your problems. A friend who understands that you need to spend time with someone, who won't ask how you are doing, is invaluable. An expert conversationalist can help you forget your pain for short periods of time by introducing one topic after another. When choosing "fun friends," let them know you appreciate their concern, tell them you have a counselor to hash out your problems, and ask them to take on the mission of providing a fun escape.

## F. Get Back Into Circulation

There are times in our lives when we need to shut down and spend some time alone. However, there needs to be a balance. Don't become a social hermit by staying home alone all of the time. Venture out. Get together with friends and maintain your social ties. If you need to make new friends, then sign up for a class, do volunteer work, join an activity club, and revive your social life.

We humans can learn from the northern geese. Geese choose to fly in a "V" formation. This has been found to be 70 percent more efficient than flying alone. Just like the geese, if you choose to fly alone all of the time, you may be making your life more difficult. You will tire much easier than you would if you had some friendly help and encouragement. Remember, after all types of pain, we need to fly again and keep up with our friends. For our sake and for theirs.

***Personal notes and ideas***

Who can I reach out to?

How will I reach out?

Is there a support group for me?
    <u>Name of group</u>     <u>Place</u>     <u>Date/Time</u>

Who can recommend a professional?

Who can I count on to be a "fun friend"?


What do I need to do to get back into circulation?

# 4

# Embrace the Healing Process

## A. Acknowledging the Pain

It is natural to want to **avoid, stuff**, and **deny** rather than acknowledge pain. However, if we don't deal with the pain and loss in our lives, the pain will deal with us by coming back to haunt us one hundred times over. Denying the reality of pain can paralyze and destroy not only the person in denial, but also those nearest and dearest to the one who is suffering.

In the midst of your pain, you may be crying often, feeling confused, questioning the meaning of life and of tragedies, wondering if you are abnormal. Remember, suffering does not make you less of a person. If anything, it means you have joined the ranks of the "normal." After all, hardship and pain are a part of life.

> Not all who wander are lost.
>
> —The Author

## B. Focus on Healing

**Acknowledge** the pain, but don't dwell on it. Instead, **focus** on the healing.

For every kind of pain, there is a healing process. If you cut your arm, it bleeds, forms a scab, the scab falls off, and then your skin grows back. If you break your leg, the bones calcify, the cast comes off, and then you go through therapy to strengthen the

15

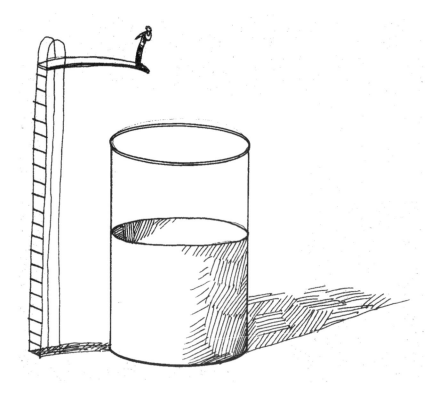

limb. It is the same with our hearts. In the process of emotional healing, three things take place:

1. You come to know **YOURSELF** better because you really have to dig down deep inside.
2. You come to know **OTHERS** better because they help you ease your pain.
3. You come to a better understanding of your **FAITH** because it works overtime during this time period.

   **EMBRACE** the precious healing process. Share it with your friends and family. There is so much to be experienced during your healing process. For the first time, some people have seen some positive consequences from their seemingly hopeless situation when they finally focus on healing. For the first time they actually felt **HOPE**!

## C. Emphasize the Positive

It's like the old question: Is the glass half empty or half full? You can see your situation as hopeless or you can choose to find something positive in it.

How would you describe this glass? Be honest with yourself. Now think about your tough situation. How does your perception of it relate to the glass? Remember, people who say "half empty" are pessimists. People who choose to see it as "half full" are optimists. Which would you prefer?

## D. Choose Your Frame of Mind

You can choose your frame of mind. Winter, that cold, blustery season, can provide an excellent example of how we choose to live our life. In many parts of the country, winter is the most inconvenient of seasons. It makes us wait, slows us down, puts us in a holding pattern. Ice storms, huge amounts of snow, and frigid temperatures can shut down a large city. School is called off, businesses close, and entertainment is canceled. It can be very frustrating to have our plans changed at the last minute. For the most part, all we can do is wait, wait until it is OK to venture out again.

So during these cold, white, stark days of winter, we can do many things to survive this frigid season:

We can complain about the cold, the snow, the days with little sunlight . . .
We can medicate our discomfort with booze, drugs, television . . .
**or**
We can wait patiently, live each day making the best of each moment, and look forward to spring.
We can see it as a glass half full. We can play in the snow, gaze upon the beautiful landscape, ski, skate, snuggle up to a warm fire . . .

Seeing winter as a glass half full is the healthiest frame of

17

mind. A positive outlook allows us to wait patiently when life is called to an abrupt halt. We won't mind the snowfalls of life. We realize that the inactivity or postponed events gives us the opportunity to recharge our batteries emotionally, physically, spiritually, mentally, occupationally, and socially.

> There is no winter harsh enough to withhold the promise of spring.
>
> —Karen Kasier Clark

And speaking of the spring: Life is like a rose. It is beautiful even though it has painful thorns. It is our choice as to whether we focus on the colorful petals and the beautiful aroma versus the painful thorns.

## Personal Notes and Ideas

Why am I avoiding the pain?

What can I do to acknowledge it?

What am I learning about the healing process?
    a. What am I learning about myself?

    b. Who am I getting to know better?

    c. What am I learning about my faith?

What is my frame of mind?

What are the wintry/challenging situations in my life?

What can I do to wait patiently?

Which aspects of my life need to be recharged?

# Part 2
# Multidimensional Healing

We are all multidimensional beings, and there are many ways we feel pain. For example, we could break our leg, lose a loved one, get fired, have friends turn their backs on us. . . . Therefore, we must take an approach that will heal all the dimensions in our lives. This part of the book will focus on the emotional, physical, spiritual, mental/intellectual, occupational, and social aspect of our lives. This theme will be further developed with respect to our reactions of denial, grief, anger, and depression. Positive solutions will be provided as to how one can process one's pain and heal multidimensionally. In addition, forgiveness and closure will be addressed.

# 5

# Health Is Multidimensional

Healthy people nurture each of the many dimensions of their lives. If we really want to heal and to move closer to being a whole person, we need a game plan. Life can be abstract and, at times, difficult to define. Imagine your life as a bicycle wheel with six spokes. Each spoke represents a different dimension.

1. **Emotional**—your day-to-day encounters with your feelings.
   a. Strong—if most things are going OK and you have a good understanding of your emotions.
   b. Weak—if you're having difficulty coping.
2. **Physical**—your body and its well being.
   a. Strong—if desease free, satisfactory weight, regular exercise.
   b. Weak—if sick, overweight, unable to exercise.
3. **Spiritual**—your relationship to a supreme being.
   a. Strong—aware of where you stand and a thirst to learn more.
   b. Weak—too busy for faith, no desire to grow.
4. **Mental/intellectual**—your intelligence and how it is challenged.
   a. Strong—if you are learning and being challenged.
   b. Weak—if not learning, just doing same things day after day.
5. **Occupational**—your means of earning an income.
   a. Strong—if satisfied with job and able to afford basic needs and certain wants.

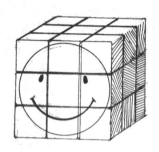

   b. Weak—if job dissatisfaction, too little income, unemployed or underemployed.

6. **Social**—your connections for companionship and recreation.

   a. Strong—if have diverse friends to meet most of your needs.

   b. Weak—don't know many people, friends have abandoned you, you've moved.

Many times the conditions of your six spokes may be very weak, but they are not your fault. Due to circumstances beyond your control, you move to a different state, get injured, or lose your job. No matter the reason, it is **your** choice to do something about it.

## A. Spokes of Life

We can use the Spokes of Life to guide us in our journey to a healthier life. Let's look at Sara's spokes. One year, she did not have a full-time job, was in very poor health, and needed to rebuild her social life after her husband abandoned her. Therefore, spokes 5, 2, and 6 are very short. Emotionally, she was a "basket case," so spoke 1 is almost nonexistent. She was doing fine mentally and spiritually, so spokes 4 and 3 are much longer, yet none of the spokes reaches the rim of the wheel. When we look at the spokes within the circle, we see which areas Sara needs to work on so her ride can be smoother.

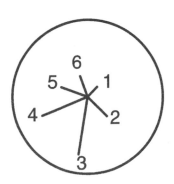

1. Emotional
2. Physical
3. Spiritual
4. Mental/Intellectual
5. Occupational
6. Social

When we make a rim that connects with the ends of the spokes (illustration below), we see how rough Sara's ride is. This illustration beautifully depicts the way we should all strive to balance our lives multidimensionally.

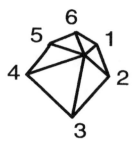

Sara reevaluates her spokes every six months. It is amazing how they change. Look at the difference between the prior year and four years later.

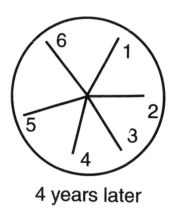

**4 years later**

Now you can draw a circle, mark the midpoint to serve as the axle, and draw each spoke as it represents your life today. Does it look like a smooth or a bumpy ride?

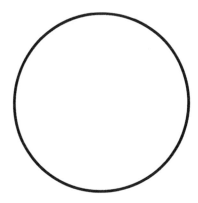

After an honest look at each dimension of your life, you can develop a plan of action to make your life more balanced. Remember, balance is the key to health.

## B. Who Am I?

Having completed the spokes of life, questions about the emotional side of our being may occur. As we mature (not just get older), we can become more aware of who we are. One way we can acquire awareness is to willingly consider the advice and wise words of true friends. The following exercise compares how we see ourselves with how our true friends see us. First, review the following list and write down the adjectives that describe you best. Next, ask one or two but no more than three supportive friends or family members whom you trust and respect to do the same. That is, they should review the list and write down the adjectives that describe you best. Then, compare the lists. What conclusions can you draw? For example:

1. How often did the words I chose agree with the words they chose?
2. Are there common themes among the lists?
3. Which characteristics (positive and negative) were chosen unanimously?

# List of Characteristics

afraid
aggravated
amazed
ambivalent
angry
annoyed
anxious
apathetic
ashamed
bashful
bitchy
bitter
bored
calm
carefree
cheerful
cocky
cold
comfortable
concerned
confident
confused
content
crazy
defeated
defensive
delighted
depressed
devastated
disappointed
disgusted
ectatic
edgy

elated
embarrassed
empty
enthusiastic
envious
excited
exhausted
fearful
fed up
fidgety
flattered
foolish
forlorn
free
friendly
frustrated
furious
glad
glum
grateful
happy
harassed
helpless
high
hopeful
hopeless
horrible
hostile
humiliated
hurried
hurt
hysterical
impatient

impressed
inhibited
insecure
interested
intimidated
irritable
jealous
joyful
lazy
lonely
loving
mad
mean
miserable
mixed up
mortified
neglected
nervous
numb
obnoxious
optimistic
paranoid
passionate
peaceful
pessimistic
playful
pleased
possessive
pressured
pretty
protective
puzzled
refreshed

regretful
relieved
resentful
restless
ridiculous
romantic
sad
sentimental
sexy
shaky
sharing
shocked
shy
sorry
strong
subdued
suspicious
tender
tense
terrified
tired
trapped
ugly
uneasy
vulnerable
warm
weak
wonderful
worried

*Personal notes and ideas*

What dimensions of my life do I need to improve?

Which dimensions are fairly strong?




How did my opinion of characteristics compare with the opinions
    of others?
                SIMILARITIES                    DIFFERENCES

# 6

# Triggers/Reminders Can Be Temporary Setbacks/Obstacles

We often get tripped up by bad memories during the healing process. Because we don't know what will trigger these memories, they usually catch us off-guard and instantly take us back to relive that painful time. However, some circumstances can be predictable triggers. You never know . . .

## A. Immediately after the Tragedy

Most people believe that the hardest time for the grieving person is **immediately after the tragedy**. It is, but people call frequently, drop off food, send cards, and make themselves very available, thereby making the first two months a little easier. The grieving person is numb to most everything, due to the amazing coping skills that our body possesses, which keep us going immediately after the tragedy. However, after the newness wears off, it gets much more difficult. People aren't as available, the phone stops ringing, cards stop coming. . . . **REALITY SETS IN!**

For example, at a dentist office, we receive a shot of anesthetic so that we won't feel any pain even though major trauma is taking place inside our mouth. As the anesthetic wears off, the patient starts feeling some discomfort.

The first couple of months after a tragedy are completely crazy, but our basic survival instincts help us to maintain during this time. After reality starts sinking in, and the anesthetic wears off, one finds that they have to start working at it. Instead of getting easier, it gets gradually harder. At this point the grieving person is no longer on automatic pilot, but needs to hold on tight and bring themselves in for a landing amidst violent weather conditions. Instead of just *making* it through the day, we will find ourselves struggling to **survive** moment by moment! Realizing that this rotten situation isn't temporary, but possibly permanent, is hard to swallow. We will need to learn how to deal with it on a long-term basis.

## B. Holidays

A common misconception is that people are always happy during holidays. If anything, the grieving person usually is more depressed during a holiday because there is so much pressure to be happy. The expectations for happiness when the person is feeling just the opposite only add guilt to the grief. Before this becomes a vicious circle for you, let your family and friends know that you just aren't able to conjure up joy and contentment. Ask them to give you some extra support and understanding, especially for those "firsts" after the tragedy—the first birthday, Christmas, anniversary, Valentine's Day, and other family occasions.

expectations

can't meet
deadlines

feels guilty

depressed

## C. Anniversaries

The anniversary of the tragedy is a tough day. That date can be haunting forever. Jessica will probably never watch the Super Bowl again. One year, while the championship football game was on television, she found her father dead in the living room. "The memories are just too painful," she said. No one reacts the same way on the anniversary date, but don't try to fool yourself and treat it like just another day. Instead, take extra care, treat yourself, do something special for someone in need, whatever it takes.

## D. Seasonal Reminders

Holidays have specific dates for which you can prepare yourself. You should feel good about getting through the holidays, but don't let that give you a false sense of security. Seasons of the year are another matter. Be aware that seasonal reminders can be just as devastating as holidays, the anniversary of your tragedy, certain places, and people.

Michele figured that if she could make it through her first Christmas after her tragedy, she could make it through anything. Her thorough and careful preparation paid off. However, two months later, she found herself often breaking down in tears even after watching a favorite sport, finishing a successful day at work, or dancing at a party. Then she realized that everything in her life had fallen apart during March of the previous year. It didn't matter that she had started her life over in a new place and at a new job, the seasonal reminders triggered her bad memories.

In a television documentary about the life of Mrs. Lee Harvey Oswald, there was a scene in which she was talking to her lawyer many years after the death of President Kennedy. She was portrayed as saying, *"I dread November. Every year it all comes back. The same thoughts, the same feelings. . . ."* So be aware that it isn't just the anniversary of your tragedy, certain places, holidays, and people that can trigger your pain, but **sea-**

**sonal** situations can be just as devastating. They really sneak up behind you without any warning.

## E. Dreams

Dreams can be tough, too. Hang in there! Over time, the horrifying nightmares will occur less frequently. These dreams, good or bad, are one way your subconscious works through your gut-wrenching experience.

## F. Triggers

### 1. Things

Anything—a sweater, a car, a restaurant, a musical instrument—can trigger sad memories. Once again, it happens when you least expect it, and you are never prepared for your reaction. While doing errands one day, Lisa saw a man wearing the exact same type of shoes that her deceased husband wore. She had not been thinking about him, but the sight of those shoes, in Star Trek terms, "beamed" her back to her past. Lisa was stunned. All of the memories and pain felt very real.

Although you can't get rid of other people's shoes, you can get rid of your own possessions that have bad associations. However, do this wisely, particularly if your financial situation is near disaster. When Lisa moved into her new home and unpacked the box that stored her dishes, the sight of them upset her. She could not look at them, let alone eat from them. So she immediately repacked them and gave them to someone who could use them. Although Lisa was financially strapped at the time, she had to replace those dishes. When she got rid of the old dishes, and bought something she could afford, she also bought sanity and peace of mind.

## 2. Images

Sights, sounds, and scents associated with the tragedy can set you back, too. Witnessing a similar situation, hearing a song from the past, smelling a certain cologne can cause you to shut down because the old feelings come back in a flash, as strong as ever. At the beginning of the movie *Man of the House*, a man walks out on his wife and child. The child's vivid memory of his abandonment is of the father waving good-bye as he drives away. Each time the child sees an arm waving from a car window, he is reminded of being abandoned by his father. Refer to page 135 for the full story.

### Personal Notes and Ideas

What or who triggers memories and feelings?

good/positive memories                    bad/negative memories

What can I do so that they don't paralyze me from functioning?

# 7

# Common Actions/Reactions

Many people attempt to heal by doing whatever they can to get rid of their pain. What they don't realize is that pain is a symptom, not the source. In order to really heal ourselves, we need to know what is causing the pain. We need to know what we are grieving.

Pain is like a river. The only way to get to the other side is to wade right through it, to plunge into the hurt, the bad memories, and the rejection. We can choose to walk along the river and ignore our pain, or we can be courageous and take the plunge to discover the cause. It is not easy. The reality of denial, the process of grieving, the examination of anger, and the possibility of depression are tough challenges. But it is worth it to come out whole and healthy on the other side.

There are many types of reactions when one is going through a painful situation. Some reactions are healthy and some are not. We need to be careful and not label someone or a certain family of being dysfunctional just because they are dealing with problems in their lives. The **situations** do not dictate whether someone is dysfunctional or not. It is the **reactions** to the situations that will cause one to be labeled dysfunctional. Doug was definitely going through some hard times after being brutally attacked by some thieves. His wallet was taken and he was hospitalized for various injuries that he sustained in the attack. He had his share of problems, but he chose to make sound decisions and react appropriately to his situation. If Doug had taken revenge, wallowed in his pity, or stuffed his feelings, then he would have been dysfunctional. Common actions and reac-

tions that can go hand in hand with tragedy are denial, grief, anger, and depression.

Before examining these four reactions to pain and tragedy, one must realize that all of these emotional states are **normal**. As previously mentioned in chapter 4, all kinds of pain have a healing process that follows. Like the cut in the arm that heals by forming a scab followed by the appearance of new skin. The body is also programmed to heal emotionally, if we **allow** ourselves to do so. Denial, grief, anger, and depression are the body's way of forming that emotional scab and regenerating the new healing cells. We all feel, love, and get attached to people and things. Therefore, the loss of anything of value to us will be devastating. The emotional healing process is a normal byproduct of pain, but it is *unique* with respect to **how** each person heals.

# A. Denial

Before understanding the process of grief, anger, and depression, the subject of denial must be understood. Denial can be elusive and tricky, as it weaves a deceptive fabric between our emotions and intellectual self.

## 1. The Reasons for Denial

There are many reasons that we go into denial:

a. Many times we cannot fathom that a certain tragedy has hit us. *"This doesn't happen in our family, it happens on TV and in the news."*
b. We have a hard time conceptualizing that a human being would do so much damage to another person, especially when it is a spouse, parent, child, boyfriend, or girlfriend. . . .
c. Denial is a wonderful self-protection mechanism. If we come to the full understanding of everything all at once, chances are that we would explode emotionally. It can be too much for us to handle all of the poisonous truth in one moment. So denial does have some benefits, as long as it isn't ignored or abused.

    1. Ignoring our situation is not healthy. When we start denying our obvious situation we will not only slow down our healing process, but put it to an abrupt halt.
    2. In addition we can abuse ourselves and actually reverse our healing process and make it worse. Some examples are: a woman who denies her pain to the point of being promiscuous, or an alcoholic who continues to deny his/her problem through frequent alcohol poisoning, are damaging their bodies.

## 2. Stages within Stages

There is a lot of talk about the phases that we go through in a tragedy (denial, anger, hurt, acceptance . . .). However, there are *stages within each stage.*

a. Complete 100% denial:
The first stage is **complete 100% denial**. The first thing we do is **deny**. We even **deny** that we are **denying** anything. *"This can't be happening to me . . ."*

b. The physical part:
Next we will start to admit things that are a little easier to accept. Such as the **physical part** of the tragedy. *"Yes, he / she is dead . . . he / she left me . . . the house burned down . . . he / she has run away. . . ."* We accept the *fact* that the people or things are no longer *physically* there.

c. Intellectual recognition:
Through various day-to-day situations, we start to **intellectually** accept things. It is inevitable. However we can choose to *ignore* these wake-up calls, or *use* them to our benefit. These precious alarms are small insignificant happenings, but they are packed with wisdom. Remember this stage is not accepting the fact that someone has **physically** left, but **intellectually** accepting how this tragedy has affected us. *"I am a widow. Because of the fire, I will never have any of my favorite photographs, clothes. Due to the car accident, I'll never be able to hold my child again."*

There will be more in this chapter about intellectual recognition during the **ABUSE** section on page 106.

d. Verbal reckoning:
During this stage we commit our intellectual acceptance to another person through the use of conversation. This may not sound tough, but many times it is nearly impossible to produce the sounds of the words:
**"rape, abuse, divorce, I am an alco-**

holic. . . ."

This is a major step in conquering one's denial phase. Yes, you will be in the conquering mode, because it is a battle!

e. Emotional acceptance:

There is a huge difference between **intellectual** and **emotional** acceptance. As one intellectually realizes the truth, no matter how excruciating it is, a false sense of security comes into play. *"I have made a great step to get through this crisis, because I have finally accepted the truth! Now it will all be down hill."*

Yes, we have achieved a great feat, but it isn't all down hill. **IT CAN GET WORSE!** As we start the final layer of emotional acceptance, we realize that the intellectual acceptance was a piece of cake compared to what we are going through now. Realizing the truth up in the **head** is one thing, but truly grasping that painful truth in the **heart** is another thing. (Refer to page 107 for an example.)

## B. Grief

The grieving process is like an onion: we need to peel off one layer at a time. This step-by-step process can be very frustrating. Just when we think we have things figured out, another layer of pain is revealed. Therefore, we need to proceed with caution, do it one step at a time, and take baby steps.

## 1. People Grieve Differently.

It is not uncommon in a relationship that one spouse or partner may immediately grieve—perhaps be despondent for an extended period of time. The other spouse or partner may "stuff" their feelings, busy themselves with projects and continually seek diversions. Later on it will finally hit them and it will hit them hard.

The sadness of this reality is that relationships often break up because people in the relationship grieve differently and at different times about the **same** tragedy.

Therefore, we need to be extremely sensitive, understanding, and compassionate to our spouse, sibling, parent, or significant other when we are sharing a tragedy.

Remember, your grief is **your** grief. Do what you need to do to process it, but don't do anything to endanger yourself or your loved ones. Honor your need for quiet times alone, but don't shut yourself off from the world. You need people and they need you. Don't let anyone tell you that you should be "over it," but do take their comment into consideration: Are you wallowing in a pity party?

There are times when you might doubt yourself: *"Am I going to be like this for the rest of my life?" "Am I just a loser?" "Can't I get a grip and go on with life?"* Don't ever doubt yourself. Be honest with yourself, dig deep, keep processing, keep moving forward, keep up your courage, make sure you do what **you** need to do.


## 2. Grief can be overwhelming.

There are times when the grief is overwhelming. In the movie *Forrest Gump*, Jenny and Forrest return to the home of Jenny's childhood. Because the house reminded Jenny of all the abuse that she endured as a child, she started throwing stones at the house. When she couldn't find any more stones to throw, she collapsed on the ground. To comfort her, Forrest said, *"I guess at times there aren't enough stones to throw"*. Yes, sometimes there aren't enough stones to throw to release all of our anger, depression, grief, and frustration. When our situation becomes this tough, when the pain doesn't make sense, we need to be willing to overcome our emotions. We need to swallow hard, be stubborn, and say, *"Even though this is so excruciatingly painful, I will survive. I will go on. I will become whole again."* (Refer to pages 134 and 135 in the Abandonment chapter for more information and healing activities for grief.)

## C. Anger: the Forgotten/Ignored Emotion

Anger is a tool for change when it challenges us to become more of an expert on the self and less of an expert on others.
—Harriet Goldhor Lerner, *The Dance of Anger*

### 1. Definition

Anger is a physiological arousal/awareness/reaction in response to hurt, frustration, fear. . . . Anger is energy that can be used for making changes. The final outcome of our anger is dependent on how we choose to use this potent energy. At the end of the spectrum, one can choose **suppression** to deal with one's anger. Meanwhile on the other end, one could use **aggression** as a means to vent one's anger. Both of these mechanisms, though very different, are quite damaging for everyone involved. More about suppression on pages 41 and 42, and about agression on page 110–112.

supression        healthy        aggression
                  processing

### 2. It's OK to Be Angry

Anger can be seen as both good and bad. Anger is good when it is a response to caring deeply about something or someone. When one cares about the children in the world, and finds out that a child has been tortured and killed, then anger is not only appropriate, but it is justified. Anger isn't always a hostile emotion. It can be protecting as in self-preservation. It can be expressed at others but meant for ourselves. It can be out of love and concern. At the other extreme, it can be out of hate. The emotion of hate and jealously can often be the same, and this type of anger is destructive! The anger of a violent jealous partner or the anger of bigotry should never be tolerated!

Anger can be connected to many different emotional states; anger means that the emotional state is very acute. It may be appropriate for us to be angry, but we need to be wise as to how and when we vent that powerful emotion. Remember most **EMOTIONS** are valid and OK. It is the **ACTIONS** that are not always OK. For instance it is OK to be really mad at someone for calling you a bad name, or stealing from you. However, it is not OK to hit, injure, or kill that person. We need to take appropriate actions and stand up for ourselves. We need to take action that won't lower ourselves to the level of the person causing our anger, or put us in jail. It is OK and **necessary** to be angry, but we need to be wise as to **how** and **why** we vent it.

### 3. Don't Confuse PROGRESS with PAIN!

Many people feel that if one is experiencing pain, then they are obviously getting worse instead of getting better, especially when it has been six months to a year after the tragedy. We say, *"I shouldn't hurt as much, because it has been a while since that day. As each day goes by, I should be getting better. . . . Therefore I am digressing instead of progressing."* Many of you have felt this way, but remember in some situations PAIN is PROGRESS! Anger, pain, and tears . . . are our indicator buttons (in sailor's terms: telltales). They let us know what's up, but only if we choose to heed the signal.

When racing sailboats competitively, the crew adjusts the lines/ropes, adjusts other parts of the boat, and looks for the wind. The skipper is in charge of steering the boat and reading the telltales on the sail. Telltales are little pieces of fabric that are attached to the sail. If they are fluttering horizontally on the sail, then the boat is being steered correctly. If they are not in this optimal position, then one needs to steer the boat differently or make other adjustments. The telltales would let the skipper know that they were not going the fastest and most efficient way

possible. Therefore in order to win the race, the skipper watches the telltales quite frequently.

In life we have telltales too. Our emotions, such as anger, tears, frustrations, are fantastic telltales/signals that make us aware that life is not going real well. Therefore adjustments need to be made. On the other hand, when we are experiencing emotions of happiness, joy, and contentment, then there probably isn't a whole lot of adjusting to do. All of us would like to have a happy and fulfilled life, in other terms, we want to win the race. In order to do so, we have to pay attention to the telltales of life. And most importantly, we need to take *action*, if we are getting negative signals.

One day Rick was building new shelves in his basement. His dog ran by quickly, bumped into the table, and knocked down Rick's almost finished shelves. The shelves were broken, but not beyond repair. Rick was so angry that he picked up the shelves and threw them down to the cement floor. Now the shelves were totally destroyed. Rick was totally dumbfounded at his reaction! After analyzing the situation, Rick had realized that he wasn't angry because of the dog or the shelves. He still had some tender spots emotionally, and his indicator button (anger) was telling him that he still had a lot of suppressed anger after being unjustly fired. Rick chose to heed the signal, seek counseling, process that anger, and put another piece of his picture puzzle back together again.

## 4. The Hog Pile (Suppression of Anger)

Don't *hog pile* your anger! Stop denying your anger, and start processing it. If you don't you will be stuck with the biggest "hog pile" of anger that will almost be impossible to remove. It definitely is **not fun** to take an honest look into one's anger. It can even be excruciating at times. It is astonishing how many people choose to start their healing process without engaging in this very important aspect. It is very unhealthy, much less dangerous, for someone to shove their pain in a closet and close the door. If you are hoping that your pain will go away by itself, you are sadly mistaken. Pain needs to be confronted, dealt with, and processed.

Don't be amazed if you find that you are real angry, or that you will cry until your eyes get puffy. You may not only be working through your recent pain, but some other ghosts from the past may be coming out too. Even though this is painful, welcome it. The more you get out, and the more you work through, the healthier you will become!

Weep what you must weep,
not only for this loss,
but for all other losses
you have sustained in this life.

—Rusty Berkus

There are people who, unconsciously or out of innocent ignorance, don't deal with their anger. They refuse to work on their anger when they become aware of it. These people seem to enjoy their pain and choose to **be** and **stay** victims. They want to harbor all that anger so that they can continue to feel the pain. In doing so, they think that they will receive pity and attention. It is amazing how many people choose this unhealthy way of drawing attention to oneself. They wallow in their pity, make sure that everyone sees their pain, and many times over exaggerate the actual truth to the situation. Remember, we may not be responsible for the *pain*, but we are responsible for our own *misery*!

## 5. Reprogramming Ourselves to Better Handle Our Anger

Many people have had to do a lot of reprogramming in their lives so that they can effectively vent their anger. Anger can be a positive tool for us as we continue to sculpt ourselves into better human beings. There are many ways to vent anger:

Hit your pillow as hard as you can and scream at the top of your lungs.
Write a letter to the person with whom you are angry. You can mail or rip up the letter.
Draw your anger, paint your pain, sketch what you look and feel like when you are angry.
Do something physical—run, swim, smash tennis balls.
Blow off steam by telling a trusted friend about the situation that has made you angry. Hopefully, they will listen patiently and then say, "I'd be mad, too!" Just being able to communicate your feelings can help you process and get rid of the anger.

Anger can be used to better our lives. After all, we are responsible for ourselves and our actions. If we want to become healthy, we need to take a look at our anger, admit that we are angry, and commit to processing it. The following are some steps to follow:

1. Identify your anger pattern. Are you a:
   - passive reactor who ignores and brushes off anger?
   - active reactor who immediately fires off and needs to deal with anger now?
2. Determine what kind of attribute you choose to have when angry:
   - Positive—anger motivates you to find the wrong and make it right.
   - Negative—anger motivates you to use revenge, slander, and abuse.
3. Realize that people are different and value things differently.
4. Identify what or who is making you angry. What or who is the real source?
5. Determine what or who will control your life and your anger. Will it be violence, abuse, alcohol, other people, or will you take control?
6. Choose the most appropriate response to process your anger.
7. Express your anger, both emotionally and physically. It may be wise to do this in the presence of a friend or counselor.
8. Let go of the anger. Process it and go on with your life. Don't allow yourself to become bitter.

## 6. Anger and Attitude

Anger can be good, but it also can be destructive. We all have the right to our own anger and opinions. However, when that opinion turns into a **nasty attitude**, then this is where we need to draw the line. Accept and respect opinions. Reject and don't be a part of any unhealthy attitudes, because they don't heal.

**Attitude** has a lot to do with healing. There was a real-life movie about one woman who was wrongly imprisoned for sixteen years for a murder she didn't commit. In addition her innocent husband was killed on death row for that murder. When asked how she survived solitary confinement, her response was, *"I realized that I couldn't change the surroundings or the situation, but I could change my attitude and outlook of the situation to SURVIVE!"*

Believe it or not, she was not in denial. She knew exactly where she was! However in order to survive, she needed to have an attitude adjustment. This conscious choice on her part is the major reason why she survived her ordeal.

Deal with your anger, don't deny it, but make attitude adjustments. It is the only way that we will make it/survive in this world. (Refer to page 107–108 in the abuse chapter for more information on both anger and depression.)

## D. Depression

Depression is a natural response to a tragic set of circumstances. It is OK to be depressed during those down times in life. It would be unusual not to be. However, it is not OK to be depressed and not do anything about it. It is not OK to wallow in self-pity, to give up, to accept that situation as a permanent state of mind. It takes a courageous person to acknowledge depression and to dig down deep into the painful inner self.

Dealing with depression can be a useful, productive vehicle to bring us back to healthiness and wholeness. In a way, depression is confusion. Confusion breeds questions. Questions breed

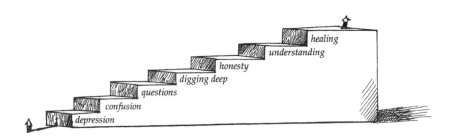

47

digging deep. Digging deep breeds honesty. Honesty breeds the understanding. And, the understanding breeds healing. THE PEOPLE WHO HAVE A PROBLEM ARE THE PEOPLE WHO SAY THAT THEY DON'T HAVE A PROBLEM, because they are too afraid to take the time, effort, and courage needed to address their inner needs.

There are a variety of ways to treat depression. It often is best to do all of the following:

Take care of yourself by eating right and exercising.
Seek counseling to help you dig for the answers to the many questions bred by the depression.
Seek medical advice to determine if the depression is related to a physical condition.

Public opinion says chemically depressed people lack emotional stability. In fact, chemically depressed people often lack various substances that the body needs. If you suffer from a brain chemical deficiency, you are not alone. Chemical depression affects millions of people, and it can be treated.

**Personal notes and ideas**

What am I denying?

Why am I grieving?

How has this pain affected me?

What makes me angry?

How do I deal with anger? Have I processed it?

Am I depressed? Do I know someone who is?

What can I do to deal with depression?

# 8

# Some Things That Can Help

Weather, natural disasters, other people's attitudes and actions, accidents, diseases . . . are some examples of the many things that we can't control. Even when it seems like life is spinning out of control, we *always* have control over our *attitudes* and our *actions*. Most people who are experiencing tragedy can feel inadequate, overwhelmed, depressed, hopeless, etc. . . . However, the greatest gift that you can give this person is the fact that they *do* have *some* control. When they realize how powerful this control is, they will no longer feel inadequate and hopeless. This knowledge of control helps to ease the depression and the overwhelming feelings. Yes! All of you, no matter what your situation is, have control of your *attitude* and your *actions*.

Here is an example of an athlete named Kelly. Kelly has torn all the ligaments in her knee one month before the state championships. She will be out for six months. There are many ways that she can react, but let's focus on two different reactions.

*Reaction #1*—Kelly gets very frustrated with her injury and her terrible luck in missing the state championships. She decides that life isn't fair and chooses to wallow in her pity. After school she goes straight home, finishes her homework, and then watches TV. She has decided she will spend her time watching television until she is well again.

*Reaction #2*—Kelly is definitely not thrilled with her injury, however, she decides to go to every practice. She wants to help the coach any way she can. She also wants to help her teammates get psyched up for the big tournament. When Kelly is not at practice or studying, she spends her time exercising the rest of her healthy body. Kelly also does rehabilitation exercises with her bad knee so that she will get back to full strength as soon as possible.

It is the same knee, in other words, the same problem. However, completely different *attitudes* and *actions*. Yes, *everyone* has a choice on how to feel and act. We may not like the choices, but we all have to make our own decisions. What do you need to do so that you can have a positive attitude and follow through with good actions?

People grieve differently from one another, therefore using different ways of healing. Here are some suggestions to consider in order to find the combination that works for you.

## A. Journaling

Keep a journal to describe your emotions, new events, revelations. Be honest with yourself, and you will have a valuable record of your journey of healing. Write in the journal when you need to. Don't feel guilty if you don't make an entry each day. Set aside the back page to list the various goals you have set, worked for, and achieved. For a boost on long, hard days, look at this list of positive things you have accomplished. It is so easy to focus on the pain, that we need to make an extra effort to see the positive.

## B. Artistic (and Not So Artistic) Expression

Express your pain in a collage, a drawing, or a painting. Be honest and be graphic. Use words, pictures, symbols, colors to describe your pain. To counterbalance the pain, make another collage or piece of art that makes you happy. Use images that make you feel whole, that make you smile, that give you hope or renew your faith.

51

## C. Find a Good Listener

Verbalizing your pain is one way to understanding it. Find someone who will just be with you, listen without offering solutions and advice, provide a shoulder for you to cry on, cry with you, hold you when you need to be held.

## D. Faith/Spiritual Dimension

The spiritual dimension of life is a source of energy, motivation, inspiration, explanation, and peace. Believing and trusting in a supreme being is a form of hope. Tragedies/crises can shake the very foundation of a person's faith. People often wonder why something so terrible is happening to them. However, as we grow through our healing process and learn more about ourselves and others, we recognize that we have gained wisdom and strength. That recognition may result in an even stronger faith.

The self-doubt and confusion that goes hand-in-hand with life's challenges can be an opportunity for spiritual growth. Admitting our confusion to ourselves and to others is freeing. An honest expression of confusion is an opportunity to question many things. Seeking answers causes us to dig deep within ourselves. Confronting and accepting what we find can be a challenge that requires a previously untapped honesty on our part. Once we face that challenge, the healing process begins. The result is a new understanding, which was born out of the initial confusion.

The healing power of a supreme being, friends, nature, or meditation doesn't remove the pain from our life, but it can help us cope with the pain and the situation that caused it. During times of despair, the presence of the spiritual dimension can be the compassion and comfort that we need not only to survive but also to grow to enjoy life again. The spiritual presence does not calm the storm, but it calms us so we are able to endure the excruciating pain of the healing process. We may not like the process, but hopefully we will like the product—the wisdom and strength to deal with difficulties.

With this new strength, we are able to help others. After struggling through a particular tragedy, one often meets someone who is going through a similar experience. It is a wonderful feeling to be able to comfort someone else. When we can tell another person we know how he or she is feeling, it makes us feel that our pain wasn't all in vain and it makes the other person feel less alone.

## E. Visualization

Take time each day to watch yourself heal and to see yourself fully healed. Close your eyes, take some slow deep breaths, and relax. Picture yourself as you are right now. The image might be of you beaten down and bruised, or collapsed and unconscious, or as a jigsaw puzzle with pieces flung all over the floor. Next, picture yourself as healing. Take time to visualize each stage—of bones and bruises healing, of regaining consciousness and becoming stronger, of the puzzle pieces being picked up and put back together. Finally, picture yourself as whole again. Don't give up hope. Don't doubt that it will happen.

Pam was a swim coach whose career ended when she suffered chlorine poisoning that scarred her lungs. She became depressed because her lifelong dream of coaching was destroyed, she was scared about her financial future, and she feared she might never recover fully. By following the physical healing regimen of medication and vitamins, eating right, drinking fluids, she had healed about 80 percent but no further. Pam tried visualization to complete her healing. She was inspired by the book *Love, Medicine and Miracles*, by Bernie Siegel, a book about terminally ill people cured by visualization, art therapy, and self-affirmation.

Pam imagined that some cute little coal miners were helping rid herself of her toxicity. They were short, chunky, bald guys with mustaches, picks, and wheelbarrows. They entered her body through her esophagus, made their way through her stomach and intestines, and out the other end. Bit by bit they picked away at all the toxic cells, put them in the wheelbarrows, and wheeled those cells out of her. Finally Pam's healing was complete, due to her persistence with visualization and self-affirmation.

## F. Self-affirmation

There are too many people and situations in this world that tear away at our self-concept. We all need affirmation, and we need to learn how to affirm ourselves because we can't always count on others to do it for us. Self-affirmation is a constant process that is key to achieving complete healing.

The mind is a powerful controller, so get into the habit of feeding it positive statements. Make sure they are totally positive. Remember that positive reinforces positive and negative reinforces negative while you compare the totally positive, not-so-positive, and the destructive lists below.

| A. Totally Positive | B. Not-So-Positive | C. Destructive |
| --- | --- | --- |
| I am doing it. | I won't quit. | I can't do it, I'll quit. |
| I am getting over this. | I won't bow down. | This is impossible. |
| I am healing. | I won't get sick. | I'll never get better. |
| I am becoming whole. | I won't be broken again. | I can't cope. |
| I am happy. | I am not sad. | I'll never be happy. |
| I am going to win. | I am not going to lose. | I'm not going to try. |

Column "A" and "B" basically say the same thing, but set "A" is totally positive. The "B" column is good, but the "A" column is better. Notice how destructive Column "C" is to ourselves and our healing process. Remember, positive reinforces positive, and negative reinforces negative. See the drawings below:

As described in chapter 6: Health is multidimensional. We need to continually reaffirm ourselves and even **attack** each dimension of our life. Try some of these affirming statements, especially in the areas that need the most work.

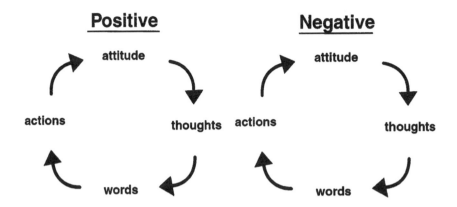

**Positive**     **Negative**

attitude     attitude

actions     thoughts     actions     thoughts

words     words

## Emotional:

1. I am O.K.
2. I am stronger today.
3. I will read a funny book today and laugh my heart out.
4. I will journal my feelings today.
5. I am continuing to heal today.
6. I am happy (or I am getting happy).
7. I know I will heal and be happy again someday.
8. I can do it on my own.
9. I'm doing the best I can.

## Physical:

1. I'm getting stronger each and every day.
2. I will walk around the block today.
3. I will jog around the block today.
4. I will run around the block today.
5. I will take my vitamins and drink lots of fluids.
6. I have energy, and I can make it through this workout.

## Spiritual:

1. I am ready to learn how my faith can help me heal.

2. My faith is getting stronger day by day.
3. My faith is helping me to heal.
4. I am growing in my faith.

## Mental/Intellectual:

1. I will read the newspaper today and learn something.
2. I will go to the library and research something I don't know much about.
3. I will enroll in a class to broaden my horizons.
4. I will get into a healthy debate with someone about politics or an interesting subject.

## Occupational:

1. I can make the deadline.
2. I am resolving the issue at hand.
3. I am trying my best to have a productive day.
4. I will call ten people today (to get an interview for a job).
5. I will be great in this interview.

## Social:

1. I am a good, loyal friend.
2. I am kind, considerate, honest.
3. I will meet someone new today.
4. I will introduce myself to someone at the party today.
5. I will call at least five friends today.
6. I will invite a friend over today.

Other ways to put self-affirmation into practice include:

**Talk yourself into healing**. While walking to the beat of your favorite music, repeat positive statements to yourself over and over again.

**Surround yourself with positive images**. Write down

your positive affirmations and put them around your home. Tape your favorite saying to the dashboard of your car, the refrigerator, or your mirror. Draw a picture of yourself totally healed and display it in a place where you will see it often throughout the day. Hang fun images around the house or office that will bring you happy thoughts. These images can be balloons, palm trees, cows, flowers, smiley faces, and others. **A positive attitude is a choice.** These circles illustrate what happens if you choose to positively reaffirm yourself and what happens if you don't.

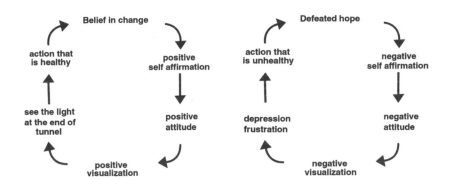

At times, it is a fight and will take all your strength and courage. But, fight the fight! Your health and well-being are worth the effort!!

# G. Expression of Emotions

Some of us were raised on *"If you don't have anything nice to say, then don't say anything at all"*. Although it's important to be considerate of others, this saying has done more damage than good. We have become experts at "stuffing" our feelings, anxieties, frustrations, anger and pain.

It is important to express your emotions during the healing process. If you don't deal with them now, you will have to deal with them later. Left unchallenged, some emotions may be almost haunting in the future. When you are in a safe place by yourself or with someone you trust, let your emotions flow. It can be painful, but let them come out, listen to them, and process them. It's OK to cry, scream, yell, fall to your knees, and sob. It can take one day or many days to process an emotion. Just be sure you are venting for the sake of venting, not to lengthen your misery. The more you get your emotions out and work through them, the healthier you will become.

After processing such painful emotions, don't forget to reaffirm yourself. Remember it needs to be positive, totally positive! The famous inspirational song was ***not***:

1. We will try to overcome.
2. We will get ourselves out of this mess.
3. We will hang in there.
4. We don't want be abused anymore!

No! It was . . . **"WE SHALL OVERCOME!"**

# H. An Inventory of Emotions

In order that we can know ourselves fully, we need to take an honest look inside. Using an emotional inventory will help in this endeavor by having us chart our experiences on paper. First, we make a tally of all the events and accompanying emotions that have taken place in our lives. Second, we take into account our reactions to those situations. Third, we look at the intertwining effects that these situations have on each other. Fourth, we can take this information and find some common themes. Finally upon gathering all the information, we can make a plan to better ourselves. Take time to do the following:

1. Do your best to write down all of the major situations in your life that left you feeling empty, sad, angry, victimized, frustrated. . . .
2. Now choose one of these situations and write down your answers to the following questions.
   a. *Who* or *what* caused this emotion?
   b. What happened. Why were you angry?
   c. How was your life affected?
   d. How did you react?
   e. What is your plan to make things right?
   f. Have you truly processed this situation. Has there been closure?
3. Repeat steps 2 for each of the situations you identified in step 1.

Here are some trigger words to help you with your inventory: (None of the words line up horizontally. It is just a random list.)

| A. Who/what? | B. What happened? | C. Life affected | D. Reaction → | E. Plan → | F. Processed? |
|---|---|---|---|---|---|
| death | accident | self-respect | denial | vent anger | vented |
| abandoned | father/mother left | self-concept | I ran away | forgive | forgiven |
| sick | heredity | future | cried | acceptance | forgiving |
| lost job | irresponsiblity | ambition | confused | grieve | accepted |
| moved | new job | financially | quit | start over | accepting |
| abused | hit by spouse | trust | questioned life | move on | grieved |
| | being used | personally | blew up | close chapter | grieving |
| | falsely accused | socially | frustrated | write letter | started over |
| | victimized | faith | hurt | confront | starting over |
| | | dignity | didn't know what | process | moved on |
| | | | to do | seek counseling | moving on |
| | | | angry | | closed chapter |
| | | | victim | | confronted |
| | | | | | processed |
| | | | | | no |
| | | | | | yes |

59

**Feel free to add more words to the previous list. It will help you with your own emotional inventory.**

Now let's look at an example of Rick's emotional inventory.

| A. Who/what? | B. What happened? | C. Life affected | D. Reaction ⟶ | E. Plan ⟶ | F. Processed? |
|---|---|---|---|---|---|
| Got fired | downsizing | financial<br>future<br>self-concept | angry<br>sad<br>hurt | process<br>find job<br>forgive | no<br>yes<br>forgiving |
| Ex-fiancee | abandoned | self-concept<br>dignity<br>trust<br>future | angry<br>victim<br>depressed | process<br>forgive<br>go on | no<br>forgiven<br>yes |
| Car accident<br><br>Whiplash/<br>broken bones | hit from behind<br><br>other driver's<br>fault | health<br>financial<br>social<br>emotions<br>future | victim<br>angry<br>depressed<br>frustrated | accept<br>process<br>go on<br>go on | accepted<br>no<br>yes<br>yes |
| Wife illness<br>and death | cancer | faith<br>future<br>financial<br>social<br>health | denial<br>victim<br>angry<br>depressed<br>frustrated<br>questioned life | accept<br>grieve<br>process<br>seek counseling<br>go on<br>learn more | yes<br>grieving<br>no<br>yes<br>yes<br>learning |

*Explanation of Rick's chart:*

1. Note that column (B) is an explanation of column (A).
2. Column (C) is just a list of as many words to describe how Rick's situation has affected his life.
3. There is a horizontal correlation to columns (D), (E) and (F).
   - For every reaction that Rick wrote down in (D), he added a plan to heal that reaction in (E).
   - For every plan Rick listed in (E), the answer to whether or not he has processed/accomplished this plan was entered in (F).

Let's look at Rick's first situation:

**RICK'S EMOTIONAL INVENTORY**

| A. Who/what? | B. What happened? | C. Life affected | D. Reaction ⟶ | E. Plan ⟶ | F. Processed? |
|---|---|---|---|---|---|
| Got fired | downsizing | financial<br>future<br>self-concept | angry<br>sad<br>hurt | process<br>find job<br>forgive | no<br>yes<br>forgiving |

- Column A. shows us that he was fired from his job.
- Column B. explains that downsizing was the reason for his dismissal.
- Column C lists that his life was affected financially, his future was uncertain, and his self-concept was diminished.
- Columns D, E, and F show us that:

- Rick is angry about his mistreatment. His plan is to process it, but he has not.
- Rick is sad about losing his job. His plan is to find one, and he has done that.
- Rick's feelings are hurt. His plan is to forgive. He is in the process of forgiving.

When you finish the inventory, look for patterns of behavior to help you understand how you react and cope with troublesome situations. In the example you will find that Rick's finances, self-concept and future have been affected the most. In addition, Rick hasn't processed his anger, has been a victim, and has had some trouble with forgiveness. Finally, you will see how well Rick accepts, grieves, and moves on with his situations.

It takes a lot of time, energy, and emotion to thoroughly finish this task. You may need to start it on one day and come back to it the next. Add new situations and revise some of the finished ones. Take your time. Don't rush. There isn't a time limit. You may be amazed to discover how much pain you have dealt with and how much you still need to process.

***Personal notes and ideas***

What things do I have in control in my life? What don't I control?

Am I able to express my emotions through writing or artwork?

Who could be a good listener when I need one?

How can my faith help me?

What are some visualization techniques that can help me heal?

What are some self-affirmation statements just for me?

Do I express my emotions? How? What are some productive ways for me to express them?

What have I learned from my emotional inventory?

# 9

# Closure

## A. Intellectual versus Emotional Closure

There are many types of closure, and we need to go through the *motions*, so that the closure becomes a reality for us. On December 23, Rick wrote a letter summarizing his feelings when he was abandoned by his fiancée seven months earlier. This was Rick's way of showing that he **intellectually** accepted his situation. Then on July 15th, he had a burial ceremony with that same letter to prove to himself that he had **emotionally** accepted his painful situation. It will be different for each person, but we need those days of reckoning in order that we can move forward with our lives. When is it the right time? The time is never right. We know that we have to do it, but to *actually* do it is another story. This is the same as getting married, having a baby, forgiving someone, trusting in a new relationship, etc. . . . Only you know when the time is right, or more properly stated, *when you can muster up the energy and courage to do it!* No one else can tell you when it is time! Is there a formula, a certain number of months, or a certain amount of counseling sessions? NO! Your healing will take as much time as it needs to take.

Bringing a closure to pain is a step-by-step process. There is not one large closure that ends our grief, but a series of small ones that move us on toward a new life. It is similar to the onion effect of the grieving process discussed in chapter 7, page 36. It is also like turning pages in the book of your life. Sometimes you can turn the pages easily and quickly. Other times it is very hard to turn the page. However, you need to examine and turn each page in order to get to the end.

Closure does not mean that we will never again feel the pain, but the intensity lessens as time goes on. It is like an appendix operation:

1. Immediately after the operation, the hospital surroundings and frequent sharp pains give you the unfortunate and consistent reminders of your situation.
2. A week later at home, the reminders are less frequent due to being home and staying busy with odd tasks.
3. As time goes on, you have almost forgotten about the operation, except for the occasional reminders of medical bills or twisting your body incorrectly.
4. Then many years go by and you have nothing at all to remind you of that painful night. Then one day you are taking a shower, and you see your scar. You say to yourself, *"Oh, yeah, I had my appendix out."* This time the reminder isn't very painful at all.

It is the same with emotional closure. Over time the memory of the tragedy changes from being a *feeling* to being a *fact*. The pain becomes less acute and occurs less frequently, although it never goes away completely. In a way that is good. Complete intellectual and emotional erasure of a tragedy is unhealthy denial. We need to be reminded every now and then of a particular tragedy. It helps us keep life in perspective.

> Time has a mysterious way of kindness. It gives
> back to us what we have lost through the pain of life.
> —Anonymous

## B. Forgiveness

If the sting of your tragedy does not become less severe as life goes on, this is a signal that you haven't processed your pain. Moreover, you haven't been able to forgive because of your anger. You need to be courageous and dig deep, face the issues, process the pain, deal with your anger, and strive to forgive. Then and only then can you bring closure to your healing process and go on with life.

**The painful past: You can't <u>close</u> it, until you have <u>dealt</u> with it!**

Forgiveness can begin only when we have complete awareness of the situation. We need to know what we are angry about, who made us angry, how it affects us. If we try to forgive before we have this understanding, the forgiving will be artificial. Superficial awareness produces superficial forgiveness. Forgiveness is a process, too. So, if you aren't ready right now to forgive, that is OK. However, strive for understanding and forgiveness. The prerequisite for complete healing is to sincerely forgive the person who caused the pain.

### 1. Why should we forgive? For ourselves!

a. **Learn to forgive out of COMPASSION for yourself!** It is not an issue of becoming a doormat so that you can be abused again. Nor do you have to come to complete reconciliation with the other person. Forgiveness is not saying that what the other person did was OK and you never felt the pain. Forgiveness allows you to change your anger from the *person* to their *action*. It is about helping yourself to let go of your anger and heal.

b. **We all need forgiveness**. We all make mistakes at some time or other. A simple example common to everyone is how many times have you been driving down the road when someone pulls out in front of you and you think, *"What an idiot!"*? How many times have you pulled out in front of someone else because your mind wasn't on your driving? *"In everything do to others what you would have them do to you."*

## 2. Unconditional Forgiveness

Can we put conditions on forgiveness? No, because then it wouldn't be sincere. Forgiveness needs to be unconditional. We need to abandon our expectations that the other person will come around to our way of feeling and understanding. The fact is that person may never repent. Many times the victim has to do all the forgiving when the person at fault sits back and does nothing. Most guilty parties are extremely good at denying. They say they see the situation, but they don't. They claim to hear what is being said, but they hear only what they want to hear. It is tough on us because their denial is so obvious. However, do you want to spend the rest of life waiting for them to see the light? Believe it or not, humans have been given the capacity to forgive, no matter how horrendous the act is. It is a choice! Face it, it is never easy to forgive, because people generally are never ready to forgive. Do you want to take the chance of becoming bitter while you wait? Or would you rather get on with life?

## 3. Owning Up to Our Responsibility

Not only do we need to learn how to forgive others, but we need to accept *our* part and responsibility for each situation. A person's situation may seem to be very one-sided, but each person did make some choices along the way. It does take two to tangle. Instead of a 50-50 fault percentage, it may be as lopsided as 95%-5%. Therefore we all have to own up to our own thoughts, choices, actions, and fault in every situation. However, there are some circumstances when a person is undeniably the victim. Victims of rape, incest, random acts of violence, drunk drivers . . . are absolutely not at fault for their various situations. The victims will need to forgive their violators someday so that they can fully heal. But under no circumstance should they feel that they need to forgive themselves of any wrongdoing.

## 4. Forgiving Ourselves

We also need to learn how to forgive ourselves. That can be the most difficult thing to do because we tend to be very hard on ourselves. When going through a stressful time, it is easy to make mistakes and poor judgments. Each mistake has some consequence, often an unfortunate one. Instead of getting down on yourself, try to avoid making life more difficult by taking extra time to make decisions and try to talk them over with trusted family and friends. Most importantly, learn to forgive yourself! If you feel that this is impossible; think about it this way: how can we have the audacity to think we can forgive others when we can't even forgive ourselves?

> When you make a mistake once, you are a human being. However, if you make the same mistake twice, you are a fool.*
>
> —The Author

## 5. Forgiving versus Forgetting

Forgiving is not forgetting. It is letting go of your own resentment, bitterness, and feeling for revenge. According to Mary Hayes-Grieco, a Minneapolis counselor, *"When you forgive and remember, you grow smarter. Forgiveness is not about saying that what happened to you was right. You still help the police put the person who raped you in jail, but you can also feel unconditional forgiveness of that person."*

We can choose not to forget in order to learn from the experience and become wiser. However, choosing not to forget in order to ruin, manipulate, and control others will not lead to true forgiveness or healing.

Rev. Albert Haase, a Franciscan priest based in Taiwan, wrote, *"It takes a lot of emotional and psychological energy to*

*Author's note: Do not be discouraged if you have made the same mistake more than once. Take heed.

*keep a wound open, to keep a grudge alive. . . . The longer I allow a wound to fester, the more bitterness, anger and self-pity poison my blood and eat my heart."*

To not forgive is to become bitter. There are many bitter people walking the face of this earth because they **can't** or **won't** unconditionally forgive the other person. They may have gone through the motions of forgiveness, but it did not make them feel better because it was not authentic, nor was it unconditional. To truly for**give** is to give a precious part of yourself to others and to give yourself a chance to keep the priceless you intact. Do you want to be **bitter** or get **better**?

It is easier to forgive when we do not judge others. Remember, none of us is perfect and each of us is different. So turn JUDGMENT into COMPASSION, and HATE into FORGIVENESS! **It is easy to hate and tough to forgive!**

*Personal notes and ideas*

What situations in my life do I need to close?

How can I put closure on each of those situations?

Am I aware of everyone whom I need to forgive and the extent of the pain caused by them? List the people and the pain.

What have I learned about my situation?

What have I learned about forgiveness?

What have I learned from my mistakes?

# Part 3
# Moving Forward

Your greatest asset in moving on with your life is a positive attitude. If you are having difficulty adjusting your attitude, review your:

list of strengths and weaknesses (the Who Am I? exercise in
    chapter 5)
positive affirmations (your self-affirmation list from chapter 8)
inventory of emotions (from chapter 8)

The next step is to devise a plan of action that addresses the many dimensions of your life. After that, it is up to you to carry out your plan, to put your life in perspective, and to choose to enjoy and celebrate life.

# 10

# Moving on with Your Life!

We need to see our healing process as that of the front windshield of our car. The future is what we see looking forward through the windshield, and the past is represented by the rearview mirror. As we drive along, we need to check the rearview mirror every now and then for cars. But if we spend the majority of our time looking into the rearview mirror, instead of the front windshield, we will probably have many accidents. It is the same with life. We need to look into our past, every now and then, to keep perspective in our lives. However, by focusing on the past, we are setting ourselves up for a crash course in life filled with a lot of unwanted and unnecessary pain.

**Develop a Plan**—identify the problem, then focus on the solution.

In order to celebrate life again after a tragedy, we need to focus on *solutions* rather than dwell on *problems*. The Spokes of Life showed us our strengths and weakness while giving us a clue on how to improve our quality of life. This previous work is important, and we must follow through with it. The following plan can lead to a more balanced and healthy life.

First we need to recreate the six areas of our lives horizontally, and add the identifiers vertically:

| Identify: | Emotional | Physical | Spiritual | Mental | Occupational | Social |
|---|---|---|---|---|---|---|
| 1. The problem | | | | | | |
| 2. Ideas to fix problem | | | | | | |
| 3. Your strengths | | | | | | |
| 4. Your goals | | | | | | |
| 5. Your needs | | | | | | |
| 6. Your plan | | | | | | |
| 7. Sacrifices to achieve your goal | | | | | | |

Developing a plan of action takes a lot of time and effort. You may also choose to do it on your own. Or, to be sure you are covering everything and being realistic, you may find it helpful to discuss the plan with several people, including counselors, spouse, best friends, parents, siblings.

As you revise your plan, you may find many of your notes overlapping and intertwining. That's because the six different areas of life are interconnected. The way they combine and deeply affect each other makes each of us our own person, unique to the world.

When you have successfully carried out your plan, you will not only have healed yourself, but also have gained an inner strength because you have persevered and survived.

The following is an example of Sara's plan of action for each of her spokes. Refer back to page 23–24 with Sara's spokes for the year with her rough ride.

# Physical
## (Notice letters correlate with one another)

For instance, #1a is about the problem of being depressed. Therefore, 2a, 3a, 4a, 5a, 6a, and 7a are the ideas, strengths, goals, etc. to fix that problem.

1. The problem
   a. Chemically/clinically depressed.
   b. Severe bronchitis.
   c. Out of shape with respect to exercise fitness.

2. Ideas to fix problem
   a. Continue to get counseling, take medication as prescribed.
   b. Get lots of rest, drink fluids, take vitamin C, finish antibiotics.
   c. Start a low-key exercising program (walking), increase to a more vigorous cardiovascular training program.

3. Your strengths
   a. Very determined, a survivor, have a strong faith.
   b. Have a history of bronchitis and lung problems, so know what to do.
   c. Physical Education major, former athlete, and current coach, so know what to do.

4. Your goals
   a. Come to an understanding of depression, and achieve a healthy chemical balance.
   b. Get rid of bronchitis.
   c. Get into good physical shape.

5. Your needs
   a.
   b. Same as **goals**
   c.

6. Your plan
   a. Continue counseling. Become more educated on Chemical Depression.
   b. Get lots of rest, eat right, take medication, take vitamins.
   c. Same as—**Ideas to fix the problem**.

7. Sacrifices to achieve your goal
   a. Financially it will cost for the counseling. My time also.
   b. Financially for medication. Less social activities.
   c. None, enjoy exercising.

# Occupational

1. The problem

   Don't have a full-time job. Have a hard time paying bills, loans . . . Over qualified with four degrees, but don't have much experience with my new career. Definitely in a Catch-22.

2. Ideas to fix problems

   Keep looking for a job. Don't give up. Keep the faith.

3. Your strengths

   Hard worker, dedicated, great references, have lots of contacts, motivated.

4. Your goals

   To get out of debt, find a new career, be able to finance a house.

5. Your needs

   Full-time job with benefits. No more part-time jobs.

6. Your plan

   Continue to follow up leads, contact a head hunter, look for new possibilities.

7. Sacrifices to achieve your goal

   Give up some of my part-time jobs to allow more time to job hunt. Financially, it will be harder.

# Social

1. The problem
   a. Husband has just left me, so lost lots of friends.
   b. Working too many part-time jobs, so no time for friends.
   c. Too sick to do anything.
   d. No money to do some social things.

2. Ideas to fix problem
   a. Make new friends, spend more time with my current friends.

b. Get a full-time job.
c. Get healthy.
d. Get out of debt, save money to do things.

3. Your strengths

    a. Very outgoing, people person, well liked.
    b. Have the potential to land a good job.
    c. Lead a very healthy life: don't smoke, don't do drugs, and drink alcohol very seldom. Should recover real soon.
    d. Know how to save, and can be very frugal. So will get out of debt soon.

4. Your goals

    a.
    b. Same as **ideas to fix problem**.
    c.
    d.

5. Your needs

    a.
    b. Same as **ideas to fix problem**.
    c.
    d.

6. Your plan

    a. Find time to spend with friends, even if it is just on the phone. Tell my best friends my problem, maybe they can introduce me to some of their friends.
    b. Keep following up on leads, find head hunter . . .
    c. Drink fluids, take medication and vitamins . . . in order to have the energy to spend time with friends.
    d. Don't spend money on anything, so that I can get out of debt faster.

7. Sacrifices to achieve your goal

    a. None
    b. Financial—Quit some part-time jobs so that I have more time to job hunt.
    c. Financial—Money for medication.
    d. No treats, going out to dinner . . .

# Emotional

1. The problem
    a. Emotionally bankrupt.
    b. Positive self-esteem is destroyed. (Like a jigsaw puzzle with pieces all over.)
    c. All used up. Nothing left to give. (Like the tree trunk in "The Giving Tree")

2. Ideas to fix problem
    a. Experience the healing process.
    b. Put my life (jigsaw puzzle) back together.
    c. Learn to say **NO** to boundary violators.

3. Your strengths
    a. Had tragedy before, have coping skills, the faith, the knowledge, and desire to heal.
    b. Had to start my life over twice before, can do it again. I have my faith.
    c. Can say NO professionally, but can't personally. Am willing to learn.

4. Your goals
    a. Become whole again emotionally.
    b. Restore my self-esteem.
    c. Be able to say NO easily to boundary violators.

5. Your needs
    a.
    b. Same as **goals**.
    c.

6. Your plan
    a. Live moment by moment. See my counselor. Journal . . .
    b. Live moment by moment. See my counselor. Journal . . .
    c. Learn from my counselor. Dig down deep . . .

7. Sacrifices to achieve your goal
    a. Financial. To pay for my counselor.

    b. Financial. To pay for my counselor.
    c. Financial. To pay for my counselor.

# Mental/Intellectual

1. The problem

   Not a big one, but to just be continually stimulated intellectually.

2. Ideas to fix problem

   Read more, take classes, find friends who challenge me intellectually.

3. Your strengths

   Very intelligent. Four college degrees. Eager to learn.

4. Your goals

   Same as **The problem**.

5. Your needs

   Same as **The problem**.

6. Your plan

   Same as **Ideas to fix problem**.

7. Sacrifices to achieve your goal

   Could be financial if I take classes. Take away precious social time.

# Spiritual

1. The problem

   No major problem, but have the belief that we can continue to grow in our faith.

2. Ideas to fix problem

   Read spiritual guides, gather with like-minded people, have alone time to reflect and grow in my faith.

3. Your strengths

   My honesty with my maker and with myself.

4. Your goals

   Continue to grow in my faith.

5. Your needs

   Continue to grow in my faith.

6. Your plan

   Same as **Ideas to fix problem**.

7. Sacrifices to achieve your goal

   None, and if there are, they are worth it!

We absolutely, positively need to take care of ourselves. We are not guaranteed that others will do so. Think of your life as driving a car. When you are a passenger, you usually don't remember where you have been or how to return to that destination. If you are a driver, you can usually find your way back. You had to do all the actions of turning, stopping, and yielding. . . . It is the same with processing our own pain. You need to be at the steering wheel when processing your Spokes of Life. Each stage needs your complete and undivided attention:

*Personal notes and ideas*

What do I need to do in order to move on?

Creating a plan will help me to. . . .

# 11

# The 4 F's

Finances, Food, Friends, and Faith all play an intregal part in tragedies and the healing process.

## I. Finances

"Can you remember when times were not hard and money scarce?"

—Ralph Waldo Emerson

Financial difficulties and tragedy often go hand in hand. Severe medical complications, expensive damage to home or car, loss of income due to abandonment, or the abrupt loss of a job not only threaten financial stability, they also cause pain. If you aren't extremely careful, debt can mount quickly in these situations.

## A. Financial Despair

Your debt can become so large that you feel like you are drowning. Whether you incurred the debt or are the victim of it, one fact remains: the debt needs to be paid in full. Here are some matter-of-fact courses of action to reduce and eventually repay that debt.

- Drastically change your lifestyle. You might have to go without new clothes, dining out, or vacations for three or four years.
- Work multiple jobs. You might have to work very long hours to make enough money to put your finances back in order. Yes, you may be frustrated, tired, depressed, and very overwhelmed at times. But you can do it!
- Cut back on your social life. A life of all work and no play is unhealthy, but you might have to put your nose to the grindstone for a while. When you do spend time with friends, choose activities that don't cost anything. Movies, concerts, restaurant dinners are out of the question. Walks, card-playing, picnics need to become your social standard.
- Reduce basic living expenses by finding a roommate to share the rent or mortgage or by moving in with someone for a period of time. Obviously, you lose your privacy, but you gain some money to pay off your debt.

If you are in the process of separating from or divorcing someone, make sure that you protect yourself financially. You must protect your own credit and not be held responsible for someone else's spending. When under stress and difficult times, make sure you take care of your finances in an honest, forthright, and legal manner. That will protect you from compounding the difficulties in your life.

## B. Plan for Financial Hardship

Don't use credit cards unless you can consistently pay off the monthly balance. Do your best to refinance your debt at lower interest rates. If you have balances on several different credit cards, transfer them to the card with the lowest interest rate. Take advantage of special offers of super low interest rates, but beware that these rates usually apply to just the first six months. After that, the rate usually goes up significantly. Sometimes you can ask the company to extend the low rate for another six months. If not, be prepared to switch to another credit card's special offer. Also watch for new loan rates at your bank that allow you to refinance existing loans with lower interest.

If involved in a separation, don't be surprised if your request for a loan is denied. Even if you have an impeccable credit rating, have never missed a payment, or have never been turned down for a loan, your difficult situation may create enough doubt in the mind of the banker to deny your request. At times like this, you have to work very hard to overcome that overwhelming feeling of devastation. This is a time to remind yourself of your strengths and goals through self-affirmation.

Don't hesitate to ask for understanding and help, perhaps your banker can refer you to a credit counselor. At times your pride will have to be a low priority during times of tragedy and financial stress. For example, after her husband left, Sara was trying to pay off her debt so aggressively that she unintentionally bounced three checks. These checks for food and necessities, which ranged from $15 to $25 resulted in service fees of $35 each—$20 from each store and $15 from the bank. She was angry, frustrated, and sad that the service fees were larger than the actual check amounts. She was also embarrassed about bouncing checks, which was something she had never done before. Sara overrode her feelings of humiliation and mustered the courage to tell each store manager and her banker about the struggles in her life at that time. When she asked them to cancel the service fees, they did, and she saved $105!

There are those who have a hard time saving money and tend to impulse shop. They really have their work cut out for them during a financial crisis. It is possible that the reason for their unbalanced situation is due to their poor spending habits. One financial counselor advises his clients in this type of situation to put their credit cards in a bowl of water and to leave it in the freezer. This way if they feel the impulse to spend money and use their credit cards to finance something, they have to wait at least thirty minutes until the cards thaw out. There are times when that impulse has gone away and the person has come back to their senses, thereby, saving the person from more unneeded financial headaches.

### *Personal notes and ideas*

Five things that I will do to get my finances in order:

1.

2.

3.

4.

5.

## II. Food

If you are wondering why there is a food chapter in a grief book, the answer is that food has a lot to do with the healing process.

## A. Fuel for the Body

If you put the wrong fuel in a car, it will chug a lot and not work well. If you put the wrong kind of food in your system, you will become sick, run-down, and ineffective.

Drink 6–8 glasses of water each day.
Eat a balanced diet.
Maintain the right levels of vitamins and minerals. Take supplements if need be.
Watch alcohol intake.
Watch your intake of sugar and junk food.


## B. Food and Finances

Eat right and save money. Stop eating fast foods. Some of this food is healthy and some of it is not. All of it is expensive.

You don't have to be a gourmet chef to be able to eat right and inexpensively. Use the money you would have spent at fast-food restaurants to buy a used freezer (20 meals x $5.00 a meal = $100). Set aside one weekend each month to make huge portions of pasta, rice, chicken dishes . . . put the food in serving-size containers and freeze them. You've just stocked your freezer with healthy meals for one month. Each day you can heat and eat a healthy, home-cooked meal. There are several advantages to this system:

You know exactly what you are eating.
You save a lot of money.
You save time by not having to cook and clean up every day.

If you don't know how to cook, give it a try because:

It's time you learned.
You will save money.
You will feel better.
You can start with easy recipes, like spaghetti, a microwave-baked potato, or sandwiches. Remember the good old peanut butter and jelly sandwich!

If becoming a balanced person is so important to you, make time, energy and effort to eat right.


## C. "Food-aholism"

Some people turn to food to take away their pain. These people are "food-aholics." Their use of food and the resulting weight problem disguise the real issues that cause them pain. Counseling can help them discover the inner pain or self-concept issues that prevent them from eating properly.

To avoid the vicious food cycle:

Eat only when you are hungry—say to yourself, "*Am I really hungry?*"

Stop when you are full.

Don't drink your calories. Drink water, tea, or juice instead of hot chocolate, milkshakes, soft drinks or alcohol.

Do something instead of eating. Go for a walk, work a crossword puzzle, call a friend, read a magazine article or a chapter in a book, write a letter, and so on.

Keep healthy snacks on hand. Cut up vegetables and store in water in the refrigerator.

Realize that diets don't work. Diet has the word **die** in it. Instead of being on a die-it, try being on a live-it. Learn to eat healthy day by day. Develop good eating habits.

Remember, *moderation* not *starvation* is the key! Consider counseling to determine if your problem with food is disguising other problems that you need to face.


## D. Hectic Schedules

Stop using your hectic schedule as an excuse to satisfy hunger with fast or junk food. It is a good idea to eat when you are hungry, so take healthy snacks with you to eat during the day. Vegetables, fruit, or homemade muffins can tide you over until you get home.

## E. Metabolism versus Catabolism

If you are losing rather than gaining weight, you may be experiencing catabolism. Under ordinary circumstances, our bodies take the food that we eat, digest it, and put it to good use. This is good metabolism. When we are very stressed, our bodies may go into the mode of catabolism. In this mode, food enters the body, takes a free ride throughout the system, and goes out the other end. The nutrients and calories are not digested or put to good use. If this is happening to you, see your doctor.

## F. Take Control

Even when we can't control other people's actions or some of our situations, we can control our own actions. When our Spokes of Life aren't evenly matched at the maximum possible, we can choose to keep our healthy spokes strong.

For example, if you are:

1. Emotionally destroyed because of abuse or abandonment.
2. Occupationally bankrupt because of a sudden job loss.
3. Socially struggling because your closest friends have moved away.

You still have control of some areas of your life and your day:

1. Seek spiritual understanding.
2. Keep strong physically, be eating right and exercising.
3. Improve intellectually by making time to read something interesting.

### *Personal notes and ideas*

Three healthy, nutritional choices that I can do daily.

Three money-saving ideas I can do with respect to my eating habits.

Healthy and inexpensive food ideas for days when my schedule is very busy.

Things that are currently out of my control.

Things that are currently in my control.

# III. Friends

Surround yourself with friends whom you can always count on, and be sure you always make time for them. There is a difference between friends and acquaintances. Friends are there when you need them, in good times and bad, even when it is inconvenient for them. Acquaintances are there during good times, when they need things from you, when it is convenient for them.

We all have many acquaintances, and others who are *convenient* "friends." However, true friends, or in other words *inconvenient* friends, are fewer in number. These friends will not think twice about taking you to the emergency room at 3:00 in the morning even when they have to be at work at 6:00 A.M. They will forego sleep and whatever else to make sure you are OK. They will do anything and everything for you because they are true friends and because you would do the same for them. Consider yourself fortunate to have one *inconvenient* friend. In a lifetime, we are lucky to have as many as five. These people are a rare breed indeed, and you often find that these friends are not just like us. They may be older, younger, different in any number of ways. But the give-and-take of a true friendship is always there.

The following is a simple, but refreshing example of how children can show their loyalty through inconvenience. Ginny has a truly wonderful friend in her younger neighbor, Veronica. When Ginny is having an intense/aerobic workout with her in-line skates, Veronica accompanies Ginny on her bike. In-line skates and bikes do not go at the same speed, so Veronica has to make several inconvenient adjustments to stay at Ginny's side. They exercise over hills, on straight-aways, and around curves. Many times Veronica huffs and puffs to keep up with Ginny. Other times she slows down or stops to wait for Ginny. Some kids just take off and don't wait for others. But not Veronica. She would always adjust her speed and do so with a smile on her face. The word that sums up Veronica and all the other true friends of this world is *loyal*. Yes, it is the loyal people that you can call friends.

## A. Circles of Friends

The degrees of friendship can be illustrated by the Circles of Friends. Those in Circle A are your best friends, true friends, inconvenient friends. They are the ones to whom you confide your innermost secrets. They will do anything for you, and you will do anything for them. Those in Circle B are the people whom you see often. They are your social friends or enjoyable work associates. Your relationship is cordial and you enjoy each other's company. Those in Circle C are your acquaintances. You don't spend much time together, but you do chat with them every now and then.

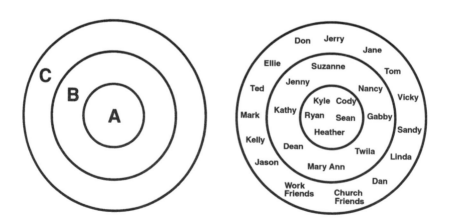

90

An interesting aspect of these circles is that the lines are not barriers: that is, friends will float from one circle to another. For example, once you get to know an acquaintance better, that person moves from Circle C to Circle B. A year or so later, that friend could move from Circle B to Circle A. It also is possible for a friend to move from A to B.

Sometimes these changes in circles are out of our control. People die, move away, take new jobs, get married. Some changes result from our own decisions. For example, if you move out of town, state, or the country, you will put a lot of distance between you and your friends. As a result, you might find some of your circles totally depleted. It's up to you to try to fill those circles again. No matter what the reason, it is tough to lose friends because we miss them and the close relationships we had with them. We need to grieve, get angry, process the hurt, forgive, and go on with our lives. Just like the Spokes of Life, we need to keep monitoring our friendship circles. Take some time to put names in the circles:

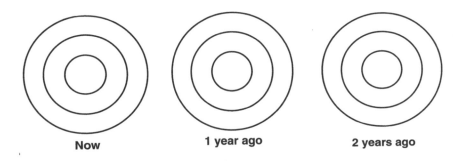

**Now**          **1 year ago**          **2 years ago**

The most current rendition of this ancient concept was developed by Marsha Forest, Jack Pearpoint, Judith Snow, and John O'Brien. They have a book, All My Life's a Circle, which outlines friendships working with circles. For information, contact:

Inclusion Press International
24 Thome Crescent
Toronto, ON M6H 2S5

91

Canada
Fax: 416-658-5067
e-mail: inclusionpress@inclusion.com
Web: www.inclusion.com

## B. Deposits and withdrawals

Relationships are like bank accounts. You have both deposits and withdrawals. If you don't have enough money in the bank, you can't do anything until you deposit more money. If you find in a particular "friendship account" that the withdrawals are outweighing the deposits by a huge margin, then you need to reevaluate this "friendship." It is not a friendship if the withdrawal/deposit balance is so diminished. It needs to be called a "convenience." Unfortunately for you, it is very inconvenient! Just remember, how can you give more to a particular person if they have withdrawn all of your resources? It may be time for some action on your part!

> Some people add to your life, and some people take away from your life. Ricky was definitely one of those who added to all of our lives.
> —Quote at funeral services for Ricky Thomas, Jr.

Just as we need to recognize our situation, we should put an end to destructive relationships also. This can be done by setting personal guidelines as to what each of us will and will not accept in a friendship or relationship. These guidelines are based on mutual respect, not on material needs. Nor are the rules based upon the amount of time you spend together or special attention. For example, Michael decided that if friends chose not to carry through on their promises, then he would choose not to put up with their selfish actions. One of Michael's journal entries shows his frustration with people whom he thought of as friends:

I've had it! I want a thicker skin. I am tired of wasting my time, energy, and emotions on people who bail on me. I have just had it! Life is too short! I guess I'm totally shocked at those who have bailed! So what if I am touchy about abandonment. Life is a choice. It is my choice to be touchy about abuse and abandonment. I refuse to be stupid and let it happen again. No way! I've got my guidelines. If people don't cut it, then forget them! As far as being my friend, I will wish and hope the best for them. However, I refuse to spend any more time with them. It is not worth ruining myself, because of their selfishness.

Not only has Michael set his guidelines, but he has also vented in an appropriate manner.

One of the most frustrating experiences is to have "friends" turn their backs on you. It is totally mind-boggling to realize that pain can be caused by our friends, not just by our enemies. You don't normally have expectations of people you don't like or people who haven't cared about you in the past. It is a terrible shock to have a person close to your heart cause you excruciating pain.

Take the time to cultivate true friends. Find people, like Veronica, who are willing to speed up, slow down, or even stop in order to be your friend.

> Friendship is the relationship we all need to help us
> through our other relationships.
> —Karen Kaiser Clark

### Personal notes and ideas

Who are my inconvenient friends? (The ones who go above and beyond the call of duty.)

Are my other "friends" taking advantage of me? If so, what do I need to do?

How are my friendship circles? Have I had many friends move into or out of circle A?

If some friends have moved out of circle A, what can I do to replenish the void?

# IV. Faith

## A. Spiritual Awakening

Spiritual awakening, which is the realization of the need for a spiritual quest, is the first step. Acknowledging the fact that your spiritual journey is an ongoing process is the next step. In pursuing our spiritual quest, we need to realize where we stand in all of this. What is our **responsibility** and what is **not**?

## B. What does faith have to offers us?

Tapping into one's faith can be intriguing, inspirational, frustrating, exhilarating, confusing, calming. . . . Spirituality encourages one to look beyond logic, reason, and facts. To believe in something that is not seen, at times doesn't make sense, yet can be a source of continual strength. Through the use of spiritual disciplines, we can find ourselves energized and empowered to not only survive this life, but to flourish in it also.

## C. Faith versus unhealthy vices.

An important responsibility for all, is to turn away from all of the destructive forces in this life. Instead of filling one's needs with unhealthy vices, one must rid themself of anything that would deter them from multidimensional health. After being abandoned or abused, one has not only been violated emotionally and physically, but also mentally, occupationally, socially, and spiritually. The pain of life's situations can lead people into unhealthy addictions. Some choose to medicate themselves on food, alcohol, drugs, work, other people's lives, instead of tapping into healthy alternatives. Before one knows it, they can be emotionally, physically, and spiritually bankrupt, because their focus has been diverted to medicating on vices. Faith can be one of those healthy alternatives.

## D. The Spiritual Quest is one aspect of our multidimensional life.

Faith should not be used as a source of "medication" to numb the pain in life. In pursuing multidimensional health, one should explore faith along with every other area of one's life. Just because one chooses to pursue one's faith, doesn't mean that one shuts off emotions and common sense. Blindly ignoring other means by thinking that their faith alone will fix everything is unhealthy! To seek spiritual advice is fine, but we have been given doctors, medical equipment, medication, counselors, exercise specialists, career counselors, friends, teachers . . . to help us in times of need.

Just because someone has a "strong" faith doesn't mean that they are immune to the pain and devastation of this world. If people are honest with themselves and their spirituality, they will hurt as much as anyone else when undergoing pain. Faith is not to be used as a **Band-Aid** that covers the pain, but the spiritual **salve** that heals the wound. Remember it is spiritual **meditating**, not **medicating**, that encourages our walk with our higher power.

## E. Faith with pain, tragedy, and suffering . . . WHY???

Many times we are unable to change the circumstances, but our faith can help us to grow. Most people who have survived a tragedy feel that the end product has been worthwhile. They don't want to go through their devastation again, but they have found peace in their emotional and spiritual growth. None of us have a discount on pain, but our faith can give us the grace to accept the pain and the strength to face the difficulties.

## F. Give faith a chance

If you are very adamant about not exploring your spiritualness, then you are missing out on a part of your multidimensional self. Don't allow your past pain or a hypocrital "religious" person to rob you of your own spiritual life. Give faith a chance!

> Don't ask . . . to have your problems eliminated, ask
> for the strength to confront them.
> —Marjorie Espinosa, 13-year-old Chilean

*Personal notes and ideas*

Where am I with my faith?

Where do I want to be with my faith?

What can I do about it?


What are the vices in my life?



Is my faith hindering my multidimensional balance in life? If so how?

# 12

# Put Your Life into Perspective

It is not what the world holds for you, but what you bring to it.

—Anonymous

Going through tough times is not easy. However, if we can put our situation in perspective and learn from our difficulties, life will be better. Many people face tragedy in their life, and it doesn't matter what economic, educational, occupational . . . status the person possesses. Pain hurts among all races, gender, culture, social class. . . . What matters is how we handle our pain and our rough circumstances.

## A. Kirby Puckett

Kirby Puckett grew up in a poor neighborhood, but through diligence and hard work, he became a great baseball player. Kirby Puckett is one of those people who knows what is important in life and what is not. Kirby's forced retirement from baseball stunned Minnesota Twins fans and the entire sports community. His class, dignity, charisma, and wisdom both on and off the field made him a hero. Kirby is an ambassador for the people.

He wasn't thrilled when medical problems put an early end to a career he loved. In fact he probably shed some tears over the situation. But he didn't become miserable either. Instead, he chose to see his life as a glass half full:

> I'm 35 years old. This is going to give me a chance to do a lot of things I've never been able to do, like be around my kids more than ever, and take them to school and take them to gymnastics practice. This is almost like a blessing in disguise. I've had so much fun. I didn't know what I was missing. I got to see my daughter go to kindergarten last Wednesday. If I had been playing, I would be in Toronto. You think things are bad, then you get to see something like that and it puts everything into perspective for you.

No doubt about it, Kirby Puckett has a phenomenally positive attitude. He knows what life is like, and he knows how to count his blessings. At the same time that he was coming to terms with leaving baseball, he was spending time at the side of his friend, Rod Carew, while Carew's daughter was dying. Kirby could retire with dignity because he could put baseball in perspective. If we learn just one thing from this, let it be to grieve what we need to grieve, to count our blessings, and to not wallow in pity, because it could be a lot worse.

During tragic times, we often wonder if our lives are wasting

99

away. However, getting to the other side of the pain can give us a new appreciation for life, and appreciation that would not have been possible without pain. For example, for people who have been seriously ill, in an abusive relationship, or suffering a series of family tragedies, *an ordinary day can be a great day* because they are healthy, free of abuse, or receive no bad news.

When life throws you a curve ball, hit a homerun!
—Anonymous

## B. A new mindset

For Ginny a day of rollerblading in the park could not be ruined by the flat tire that she found when she returned to her car. After the flat tire was fixed, a park ranger came by and said *"I hope your day gets better."* Ginny thought, how could it get any better? She had just finished rollerblading on a gorgeous day. Then she realized he was referring to the flat tire. She thought, *My day wasn't ruined! It takes a lot more than a flat tire to ruin my day.* She reflected that in past years, the flat tire would have ruined her day, but not anymore.

People who put their lives in perspective often put *an end to complaining.* Instead, they appreciate what they have. For example, someone who was unemployed for three years is much less likely to complain about extra work to be done on the job. Receiving enough employment rejection letters to wallpaper your room and wondering where you will get the money to pay the rent, are much more stressful than a stressful job.

## C. The sensitivity radar

Tough experiences also can develop a new sensitivity to other people and their emotions. Victorious survivors of pain become more patient, tolerant, and understanding when someone is hurting. When this *sensitivity radar* helps us detect when others are experiencing pain, we can show them understanding and

100

compassion. If nothing else, we can ask how they are *really* doing and then be good listeners.

We can also show our sensitivity when others are experiencing the powerful emotion of anger. One of the byproducts of processing pain is the knowledge that anger is a telltale sign of unresolved issues. When faced with someone else's anger, we need to be careful not to take it personally but to empathize and offer to help. As survivors of life's challenges, we need to be more receptive to listen, observe, and to be there for each other.

## D. Defining true happiness

Through life's challenges we can find that **happiness** is not the attainment of what one **wants**, but the realization of how much one already **has**. Too many ignore the present and expect to be happy in the future. When they get their new job, find their true love, buy their dream home . . . then they will finally find that lasting happiness and peace. Yes, these things may make you happier, but true happiness needs to come from within.

When we put our lives in perspective, it is easier to put them all together and set new priorities. Just because you may not be the image portrayed by Madison Avenue advertising executives, and just because you may not have certain possessions that *you* think others expect you to have or that you really want, doesn't make you less of a person. Get your personal values straight and put them before your material values. Balance the spokes of *your* life and you will be in position to seek and achieve your other desires.

*Personal notes and ideas*

How has my perspective on life changed for the better?

How am I going to use this new perspective to keep myself happy and fulfilled?

How will I use my newly found sensitivity to help others?

True happiness for myself is . . .

# 13

# Choosing to Enjoy/Celebrate Life

## A. Accepting that life is change.

The sooner we accept the facts of life—

Life doesn't always make sense.
Life is change.
Life is a process.

—the sooner we will be able to not only survive and function, but also live and enjoy!

> We cannot direct the wind, but we can adjust the sails.
> —Anonymous

In most sailboat races, the wind shifts quite frequently. The wind could be coming from the northwest, and then ten minutes later shift to the north. As sailors, we need to pay attention to these wind shifts. If we choose to ignore them, then we will definitely slow down and lose the race. Our goal is to have the wind hit the sail at the perfect angle, all of the time, so that we will win. In order to keep that perfect angle, the skipper needs to adjust the sails quite often. Sometimes sailors adjust the sail every thirty seconds, or so, for a two hour race! It is the same with life. We have changes sometimes hitting us moment by moment. Resisting change isn't always the best idea. Change is tough, but change can be good. We all need to remember that life is a

PROCESS, not a single EVENT. Therefore WE ARE IN PROCESS AND A BYPRODUCT OF PROCESS IS CHANGE!

> Life is a series of unscheduled events to solve a series of unanticipated interruptions.
> —Karen Kaiser Clark

## B. Choices

We have a choice. **We can make it *work* or we can make it *worse*.** The ability to enjoy and celebrate life depends not on what happens to us but on how we react to what happens. A simple, yet descriptive example of this is a hanging mobile. Imagine a mobile that is hanging perfectly with twelve various pieces in your living room. The door opens and a strong wind blows the mobile around, causing a piece to fall to the floor. Now the mobile only has eleven pieces and is all out of kilter. Once the mobile is readjusted, it can hang freely again. Life is like a mobile. Change can hit us at any time and can put our lives out of kilter. We lose things, people die or leave us, new people enter our lives, we move to a different city—but, if we make proper readjustments, we can live freely again.

The past can be a great help or a huge hindrance to emotional stability. It depends on how you choose to view it. The following holds true if you are out of your terrible situation and time has gone on. You can allow your past to control you to the point of self-destruction. Or you can see the past as a memory that no longer has any power over you anymore. As a matter of fact, the pain that you are feeling right now is just a *thought*. It isn't happening anymore, so it only has control over you if you *choose* to give it the power. If you have been abused, and the abuser has ruined a part of your *past*, don't allow the abuser to ruin your *future* too. This applies if you are in the *process of getting out of a relationship*. It also applies if you have *been out of that relationship for years*. Don't allow your past pain to dictate your present and future emotional health. Life's situations dictate whether you are surviving, functioning, living, or enjoying. Although you need to go through each stage, you get to choose how long you will stay in each one. You can have a pity party or you can start the healing. It is your choice to fight the pain, depression, hurt, rejection, abandonment, and make life fun again.

Each of us has our own "cross to bear." Sometimes it is visually apparent and sometimes it is hidden. We can allow it to ruin our life, or we can choose to have a full life in spite of the inconveniences and nuisances. Pam wrote, *"These are things that I will have to deal with for the rest of my life. But I also need to learn how to survive, function, live, enjoy and flourish in spite of it all."*

Unfortunately, this business of choice rarely comes at convenient times. Many times you will need to make decisions in the midst of searing pain. You might be feeling absolutely zapped in all areas of your life at the same time that you must make a choice to fight against depression, loneliness, tiredness, abuse. At times like this, it is imperative to remember that *being STRONG is a choice, too.* It is a moment-by-moment and a day-by-day choice. People aren't always inherently strong, they choose to be strong.

Marietta battled cancer for five years of her life. Her attitude was very impressive. Most people say that people are *dying of cancer*. Marietta was described by many as *living with cancer*. She kept doing as much as she could. Her mentality was never that she couldn't do things *because* of her cancer, she did them *in spite* of her cancer. During her five year struggle with cancer, only three months of that time period did Marietta actually start dying of cancer. However, it was the physical not the emotional part that was dying of cancer.

You can be the problem or the solution.
—The Author

## C. Winners and losers.

You can be a winner or a loser in the healing process. You can persevere and enjoy life again if you deal directly and honestly with your pain, anger, depression, abuse, and forgiveness.

## D. The dance party of life.

Life is like a dance party. Sometimes you dance, sometimes you sit out, and you may even have to switch partners. But it is imperative that you never stop dancing! Never give up on yourself or your faith. These are two very precious things that you can't live without!

107

| WINNERS | LOSERS |
|---|---|
| Never quit - prevailors | Always give up - quitters |
| Dwell on rewards, solutions, the future... | Dwell on the problems and the past. |
| Encourage | Criticize, condemn, and complain. |
| Exhaust all possibilities and create alternatives. | Stop trying, and give up easily. |
| Ask **HOW** and **WHAT** statements that talk about the <u>solutions</u>: <br><br> *"This is **how** I can do it!"* <br> *"This is **what** I can do!"* | Ask **WHY** questions that talk about the <u>problem</u>: <br><br> *"**Why** is this happening to me?"* |
| <u>Problem solvers:</u> <br><br> See how they **<u>can</u>** do it with **<u>ideas</u>**! | <u>Problem creators:</u> <br><br> See how they **<u>can't</u>** by using **<u>excuses</u>**. |

Don't let what you *can't* do stop you from doing what you *can* do.

       —David T. Lathrop

Be stubborn! Celebrate life in spite of your challenges! Children are the best examples. They will run, fall down, and scrape their knees, but they get up and start running around again. When eight-year-old Laura was learning how to skate, she took a couple of spills. After one particular hard fall on a patch of rough bumpy ice, she picked herself up said, *"I'm not going to let one stupid bruise spoil my fun!"* and she skated off. If you adopt this same mentality, you won't wallow in self-pity when you hit a rough bumpy patch. Instead you will pick yourself up, shake yourself off, and get back to the business of having fun again!!!

> Blessed are the flexible, because they will not be bent out of shape.
>
> —Anonymous

### Personal notes and ideas

List recent changes (positive and negative) in my life.

What do I need to do to readjust myself?

What kind of choices do I need to start enjoying life?

List things to do in order to enjoy life.

# Part 4
# Abuse and Abandonment

This part of the book addresses the tough issues of abuse and abandonment, and offers various ways to cope. We will delve into the multidimensional aspects for each issue. The nature of these two mistreatments are very closely connected. If you have only been abused, read the section on abuse and at a later date read the abandonment section, and vice versa. Both sections will benefit people no matter whether they suffered through abuse and abandonment or not. Moreover, if you have never experienced either mistreatment, becoming educated on the subject would be worth your while.

# 14

# Abuse

## A. Definition

Abuse is the imbalance of power. This imbalance is rarely mutual. Most abusers will justify their actions by saying that, *"I lost control of my emotions and actions...."* No, the abuser didn't lose control, they chose to use a learned behavior of violence or manipulation to prove their point. *"Domestic violence is a pattern of behavior in which one person attempts to establish control and power over another through threats and violence,"* according to Robert Geffner, Ph.D., president and founder of the Family Violence and Sexual Assault Institute in Tyler, Texas. *"It can include physical or emotional abuse, economic abuse, sexual abuse, threats, neglect, intimidation and isolation."* In addition to the forementioned types of abuse, there are various others including spiritual abuse and abandonment. For more information on the abandonment phenomenon, see the next chapter on page 129–130.

## B. The abuser

You will need to pull out all of your nuclear arms to be able to survive, let alone defend yourself, when you are being abused. Many abusers are unable break their destructive habits, but some have found help through various support groups and have mended their ways. There can be hope when dealing with abusers, but one must be very alert and be ready for the abusers' inappropriate actions. Abusers usually do the following three things:

BLAME                    MINIMIZE                    DENY

### Blaming

They will use everything they can as a weapon against you. They will prey on a former dysfunction, when it has nothing to do with the situation. For instance, you were beaten as a child. Your abuser can say, *"Well, you are just extra sensitive because of your past."* Yes, maybe you are sensitive, but their actions are not appropriate. They will blame others, the situation, the weather, the time of day. . . . One of the biggest blaming "scapegoats" that abusers use is "nagging." You are not nagging if you have an agreement with the other person and they continue to renege on their responsibility, they have continually forgotten, or have been procrastinating. If you need to remind them often, because your well-being is dependent on their follow through, then do so in an assertive manner. Be careful, these people may never take responsibility for their actions nor will they listen to you.

### Minimizing

The abusers are great at minimizing your pain. They will say, *"Oh, you are making a mountain out of a mole hill. It really isn't that bad. You are imagining things. What you are upset about wouldn't bother other people, as a matter of fact, it wouldn't bother me in the least."* If you really hurt and your conscience is telling you something, don't back off! Stay true to your convictions. They may never listen to you, but don't ever apologize for how you feel. Don't ever let them force or manipulate you to minimize your pain.

### Denying

This is huge. They just don't get it. They didn't get it before, now, and will probably never get it! Denying is a wonderful mechanism for people to feel good about themselves. It is like a security blanket that allows the person to go on without truly attacking the real problem. Denying plays a big part in blaming. In order to blame someone else, one needs to deny that they are a part of the problem. Dumbfounded by their actions, you say to yourself, *"How can they not see. It is so evident."* Abusers are great at rewriting their life's situation in their own minds. They will distort reality to the point that their lie becomes very *real* to them. They may say that they are *seeing*, but they aren't *perceiving*. Similarly, they may say that they are *hearing*, but they aren't *understanding*. Get used to the fact that there are people who **deny** rather than **accept** responsibility for their actions. They choose to **grow OLD**, instead of **growing UP**!

Abusers can be the persons whom you least expect. A woman who was beaten repeatedly for twenty years by her husband said that he was a popular police officer who was well respected in the community. *"My husband was a good-looking and educated man with a winning personality and a good job. I know of several professional people, doctors and lawyers, who answer the same description and also have beaten their wives regularly."*

We need to realize that the so-called "good guys" with great reputations can be as brutal as any other man convicted of assault. The sad thing is that many women put up with this abuse because they want to protect their husband's career, their social status, money, and every other item under the sun.

Emotional abusers are what some professional counselors calls "**nice users**." Many of them won't physically touch you, but they will damage you emotionally beyond belief. They will use you, manipulate you, make you feel sorry for them, play the victim role . . . anything so that you continue taking care of them. Most of the time, their "needs" are only **wants** masqueraded as "desperate needs." The abusers, male or female, will do nice things for you, put you on a guilt trip about their tough luck, or just be plain lazy and convince you that it is your responsibility. The abuser can be so deceptive that their victim won't even realize the abuse. People are surprised to learn that some of the nicest people can be the most damaging emotional abusers. Another word for them is "closet" abusers.

# C. Abuse and our emotions/reactions

There are many types of abuse as there are various kinds of **pain**. Most common are sexual, physical, emotional, and spiritual abuse. It is rare to experience abuse without some form of **pain** accompanying it. Abuse can have a close connection with **denial** also. One of the toughest things a person can admit is that they have been abused by a stranger or much less by a loved one. Therefore not owning up to the truth can produce a very **depressed** and **angry** person. Don't be surprised if an abusive situation has any of the following reactions that go along with it, such as, denial, pain, anger, and depression.

## 1. Denial/Intellectual recognition

At times it can very hard to come to grips with the truth in our lives. However, when it comes to abuse, each person has to see it on their own. You can tell a person, until you become blue in the face, that they have been abused. Most of the time, you will just be wasting your breath and probably putting your relationship with the abused in jeopardy. No one wants to hear that they have been abused. Each person needs to come to terms with their abuse in their *own way* and on their *own time*. You might be able to help facilitate "seeing the light" through the use of movies, television programs, books, magazines, and support groups. However, the abused person will probably realize the inevitable through their day-to-day situations. (As previously mentioned in the **intellectual** acceptance phase in the denial section of this book, page 35.) Let's look at Sara's situation:

Sara's counselor had told her in February that she was an abused wife. Sara told him **"No way!"** Then she proceeded to give him tons of reasons (excuses) why it wasn't true. Some of her reasons were legitimate, but even so, Sara wouldn't allow herself to see the truth. Sara's counselor was great! He never mentioned it again. Then one day in October, Sara marched into his office and said, *"Yes, I am an abused wife."* He then said, *"Well, it is about time!"*

Refer to page 35 about the small insignificant situations that serve as your wake-up call. Sara's wake-up call was the fact that a co-worker offered her boxes because she was moving into her new house. Sara's immediate reaction was, *"Why is he being so nice to me?"* Sara became very uncomfortable with the situation and abruptly told him that she didn't need the boxes. In the following weeks, Sara noticed that this co-worker was nice to everyone. That was when her wake-up alarm went off. He was just being nice to her like he was to everyone else. It was then that Sara realized that she had gotten so used to being treated so badly that everyday "normal" treatment was too much for her.

Yes, it was **boxes** that pulled Sara out of her denial. It was rough for Sara to accept *intellectually*, a hundred times harder to *communicate* it to other people, and a million times more difficult to accept it *emotionally*. Yes, each person needs to realize their abuse individually. **However if the abuse is brutal or can be fatal, all of us need to intervene and save the other person.** The abused person may be so battered, physically or emotionally, that they have a *sense of powerlessness* that renders them too incoherent to save themselves. Don't wait for others to do it. Take action now!

### 2. Anger and depression

**It is OK to be angry** at anyone and anything that has caused us discomfort. It's OK to be mad at your parents, teachers, children, spouses, friends, bosses. . . .

It is OK to be *sad and/or angry*, because we are just being honest with *ourselves* and *our maker*. However, we still need to believe that we will heal from the abuse that has jeopardized our emotional health. The second we stop believing and trusting, we have lost our **HOPE! And that is not OK!** Upon losing hope, we start to worry. Anxiety has no good purpose on this earth, because it causes too many physical and emotional health problems. There is a cartoon in which Ziggy is sitting in a rocking chair. The caption says, *"Worrying is like a rocking chair, it gives you something to do, but you don't get anywhere."* So yes, be honest about your emotions of anger and sadness, but don't allow worry and anxiety to get the best of you.

Anger and depression are not OK if we don't process them properly or use them as revenge against our abusers. Anger needs to be vented appropriately, and depression must be analyzed with meaningful treatment. A permanent state of either of these emotions is very unhealthy and could lead to a very dysfunctional life. Therefore you could be to blame for your anger and depression destroying your life if you choose to mishandle these volatile and controlling emotions.

## D. Abuse and your unhappiness

**No one deserves to be abused! Absolutely no one**! Even if you have done something "wrong," you don't deserve the abuse. Don't let anyone tell you, or convince you, that you are at fault for someone abusing you. On the other hand, **you have the choice as to how *long* the abuse and unhappiness endures.** Remember that an abuser is *only* effective if they have someone to abuse. An abusive relationship can be labeled dysfunctional, but it is still a relationship! It takes "two people to tangle." So if a person doesn't do anything about their abusive situation, then they are ultimately responsible for their unhappiness. Many people have gotten out of abusive relationships and are proud of themselves for seeing the light and getting out! You can too!

## E. Letting go/getting out

Living with an abuser is incredibly hard for some, if not impossible. Knowing an abuser is tough, but you don't have to live with them. This makes it somewhat easier, because you don't have to share living space with them. However, when you are married to one, you are really stuck between a rock and a hard spot. You have to go home daily, to that house or apartment that you share, until you decide to get out. You need to get out to save yourself, but most people also take their vows very seriously.

No other person in this world is worth dying for when it is a situation of abuse. Some women are too ashamed to report the abuse, because they are trying to save their marriages for the children's sake. Many religious women take their vows seriously because it is an integral part of their faith. They said and still say, *"I promised that I would stay with my husband no matter what . . . until death do us part."* But the question is until *whose* death . . . **yours**?

Sara really struggled with breaking her vows. One day when Sara was talking with her counselor, she asked, *"How can I break my vow? I took this vow seriously."*

Her counselor's reply was, *"Now wait a minute. Yes, vows are to be kept sacred and should be upheld. But this is when the relationship is like 'normal' marriages where you struggle, argue at times, and get frustrated. . . . This doesn't apply in abusive situations, where the abuse is serious and the abuser is unrepentant and unwilling to go get help or change."*

LETTING GO is the toughest thing an abused person can do, but it is imperative for their survival! Definitely the most excruciating pain came when Sara had to let go as her husband self-destructed, knowing there was nothing that she could do but sit back and watch. People can encourage the abused person to get out, but only the abused know when the time is right. Drawing the line is a tough thing to do. When do we say enough is enough? One day it became pretty clear to Sara that when it gets to the point that your <u>DIGNITY</u> is being <u>RAPED</u>, you need to see your situation for what it is worth and <u>GET OUT</u>! **Every person has been given their own dignity, and no one else will protect it but that particular person**. As tough as the decision may be, don't allow anyone the opportunity to rape you of your dignity. No other person or situation is worth losing your dignity in order to be with them.

## F. Putting up your boundaries

Caretakers, beware! You could care-take yourself to your own grave. Caretakers want to believe in people, give them the benefit of the doubt, and help them through their trials. Caretakers usually empathize, *"This person is acting this way because they have had it real hard. So we need to be understanding."* There is some truth to that. However, caretakers must learn the importance of boundaries and the need to reinforce them *daily*! People who continually take from you are called "boundary violators." Caretakers, on the other hand, are giving, and they would never think of using people. Therefore, they have a false sense of security that it won't happen to them. WRONG!!! It happens all the time! Just because you won't use people doesn't mean that other people are as conscientious as you are. BEWARE!!! You need to thoroughly think through this issue:

## MY BOUNDARY CHART

|  | FAMILY | FRIENDS | WORK |
|---|---|---|---|
| My weak points. |  |  |  |
| Do I say no? |  |  |  |
| How can I be manipulated? |  |  |  |
| When to draw the line? |  |  |  |
| How to draw the line? |  |  |  |

1. What are your weak points?
2. Can you say, NO?
3. How can you be easily manipulated so that you give more of yourself, finances, or possessions than you should?
4. When should you draw the line?
5. How do you draw the line?

The following is a worksheet for you. You can answer the questions generally, or you can specifically write in people's names and answer accordingly. For example, you may be surprised to find out that you don't have any problems with boundary violators at home, but you have friends and co-workers who constantly use you or vice versa. Check for patterns in this chart.

Many people have allowed boundary violators into their lives and should rethink, reprogram, and implement new procedures to protect themselves.

1. **We need to be *assertive* and not *aggressive*.** Being *aggressive* means that one uses inappropriate means to get your point across. Their disrespectful actions are evident by being selfish and not considering the needs of the other person. On the other hand, being *assertive* means that one uses low-key approaches to convey one's point. They are not being obnoxious, but they are "cutting to the chase." They are taking a strong stand, but they are not intimidating, nor disrespectful to the other person. When we need to confront people, we must be assertive, not aggressive.

For example, Jack is helping Bob out of a tough situation. Jack lets Bob stay in his house for free until Bob can afford a place on his own. At first it is great, and Bob is very grateful for Jack's generosity. Bob helps around the house and isn't a bother at all. Then all of a sudden the tables turn. Bob not only stops cleaning, but he has become very sloppy. To make matters worse, Bob starts asking for extra favors, which are definitely out of line. Bob becomes indignant because he isn't getting his way. Well, there are a couple ways that Jack can confront Bob.

121

a. **Aggressive** actions would be:

1. Attacking the person verbally. *"You lazy slob, ungrateful jerk, get out of this house immediately."*
2. Physically harming them.
3. Spreading vicious rumors . . .

b. **Assertive** actions would be:

1. Creating a written agreement with respect to the living arrangements.
2. Confronting the person truthfully. Using "I" statements instead of "you" statements.
3. Discussing the consequences if the contract is broken.

2. **Boundary violations**. People can be controlled by another person and not even know it! So let's brainstorm on some ways that your boundaries can be violated. The other person will:

a. Be constantly late.
b. Say and not do.
c. Make and break promises.
d. Guilt you into doing something.
e. Do things without telling you first.
f. Lie and cheat.
g. Constantly put their needs first.
h. Manipulate you into feeling sorry for them.
i. Continually blame you and not take responsibility for their actions.
j. Borrow money and not pay you back.

And the list goes on . . . please add:
k.
l.
m.
n.

3. How can you protect yourself from boundary violators.

a. Look at their **actions**, not their **words**. Don't always be trusting and think, *"Well, of course I would hold true to my promise. . . ."* Even though you would always follow through, doesn't mean that they will.

b. Be honest in your evaluation of them. It is nice if we could give the person the benefit of the doubt, but we also need to be realistic! For example just because an abusive alcoholic stops drinking, doesn't mean that they have automatically stopped violating your boundaries and using you. On the contrary! They may find some other way to manipulate, deceive, and confuse you. It is great that they aren't drinking, but they need more rehabilitation before they get the privilege to spend time with you. Note the word *privilege*! You need to see it that way! You also need to see people for what they are really worth.

c. Realize that the person may seem like they really want to do it, but cannot follow through with their desires. They may have the *sincerity* but not the *ability* to make it happen. They may choose to keep themselves slaves to their dysfunction.

d. Ask yourself if these people, who say that they can't do something, are truly unable to do it. Is it that they **can't** or **won't**? Realize that some people weren't there and couldn't be there. In addition they *won't* and *can't* be there in the future. If this is your friend, you need to re-evaluate calling them a friend. You may need to call these people wimps! Wimps are:

> W eak
> I mmature
> M anipulative
> P eople (who are)
> S elfish

e. Learn to **say no** and don't feel guilty about it! Learn to not only say NO to drugs, but also to boundary violators. BEWARE!!! Most abusers manipulate you into helping them. They feel entitled to continue receiving that special treatment. You start doing nice things for them, they get used to it, and then they take advantage of our kindness. There are times when our kindness can become enabling to the other person. Enabling another person is taking care of them to the point that they don't need to take responsibility for themselves or their actions. Basically, an enabler keeps cleaning up the other person's mess, therefore taking the other person off the hook, so as to speak.

We need to stop the vicious circle. We must stop making it easy for the abusers. Many times we choose to feed their habit, rather than say "NO." When we choose to enable the abusers, by taking responsibility for their actions, we allow the abusers to continue their abusive ways. Therefore the enablers become more victimized. Upon receiving more abusive treatment, the enablers' self-concepts diminish. They start to feel like they aren't worth much due to the abuse that they are enduring. An unhealthy self-concept leads to clouded vision on the enabler's part. Many times the enablers start believing that they are the reason for the problems. So they don't stand up to their abusers and the vicious circle repeats itself. See the diagram below:

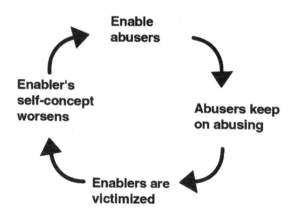

**Enable abusers**

**Enabler's self-concept worsens**

**Abusers keep on abusing**

**Enablers are victimized**

If we continue enabling them, they keep on expecting these nice gestures, start taking them for granted, and don't get it when you finally have the guts to stop. Read the children's book, *The Giving Tree* by Shel Silverstein, which depicts co-dependence, entitlement, using, and blind unconditional giving. This unhealthy relationship between the boy and the tree goes to the point that the giver (the tree) has nothing left to give. The story ends with the tree becoming a stump. If you continue in an abusive relationship, you will become a stump!

## G. Some types of abuse

### 1. Spiritual Abuse

It sounds uncanny to think that there is something called Spiritual Abuse. How can this be? It is the last place that you would think that abuse would happen. Church, religion, . . . are supposed to be healing and soothing to our aching souls. People go to spiritual ceremonies, leaders, and group studies to relieve their pain. So how could there be pain in religion? Well, there is pain and it is prevalent in many societies, cultures, denominations. . . . Most of the time, the abuse is unintentional where people mean well, but they have taken things out of context. However, there are times when the spiritual abuse is intentional and the person is well aware of their actions. The main reason for this abuse is not that your higher power has let you down, but that man has errored. Man has stretched, manipulated, over theorized, not changed with the times, interpreted falsely . . . some spiritual doctrine.

### a. Inclusiveness

Our world is filled with many diverse cultures, which each have their own needs, mores, traditions, and expectations. In order that we might co-exist peacefully on this earth, a sense of unity must happen. This unity is not only **tolerance** of other's differences, but the **acceptance and appreciation** also. We don't need to agree with everyone and their choices, but we do need to put into practice **all-inclusiveness.** This nonjudgmental attitude should not prevent people from continuing to love, follow, and devote their life to their higher power. People who are OK with themselves and their spirituality may not agree with everything, but they are accepting and not condemning.

### b. We need to keep it in perspective.

In a major tragedy, many religious people choose to *only* tap into their spiritual side. They profess that they are going to trust their higher power to take care of everything. Now the mind set of totally trusting in your maker can be beautiful. However, our creator has given us many resources to aid in our healing. Maybe we will need to go to a psychologist, medical doctor, career counselor, nutritionist, allergist, teacher . . . to become fully healed. According to Dr. Larry Crabb, a renowned author on religious issues, some approaches are lacking in encouraging a real honest look inside of the person. Therefore, superficial change is the by-product. He advises that a deep change is imperative. He states, *"The tragedy is that counselors (not connected with any spiritual affiliation) are often more aware of the importance of facing who we are than the churches."*

Most religious people are taught to live by **faith** and not **feelings**. If this mentality is not kept in perspective, one could become emotionally inept. We have been given some amazing self-regulating mechanisms for all dimensions of our lives. For instance, we won't keep our hand on a burning stove due to our physical receptors. We need to keep all receptors functioning, especially the emotional ones. If we don't feel our pain, we aren't giving our faith a chance to work.

To struggle in your faith can lead to an incredible experience with your spirituality. Yes, we should be appreciative for what we have, but when we hurt, we need to cry, get angry, scream at the top of our lungs, and say OUCH! Being real is what our faith is all about.

## 2. Relational abuse.

Abuse definitely goes two ways. The difference between partners in **abusive** relationships is:

| | Abusers | Abused people |
|---|---|---|
| **Responsibility** | Take responsibility for **nothing**. | Take responsiblity for **everything**. |
| **Actions** | All lip service<br><br>Say it, maybe even mean it, but don't do it. | Lip and service<br><br>They hold true to what they say. |
| **Images** | **PRESENT** images as if they are doing it, or are going to do it. | **PAINT** images: What is wrong with this picture? |
| **Controls** | Will use the "controlling". issue to discredit the other person. They will rationalize their behavior. | Will need to institute controls for the lack of responsibility on the other's part. Need to implement damage control for the other's lack of action. |

Now we will discuss the typical abuse that goes on from man to woman. *Yes, the roles can be switched and the abuse can go from woman to man.* If that is your case, please read this next chart and switch roles as you go along.

To make it in life really isn't an issue of gender, but taking responsibility for one's actions. For instance being *male / female* is a matter of birth, but being a **man/woman** is a matter of choice. In addition, any one can bring a *baby into this world*, but it takes dignity, responsibility, selflessness to be a **mother/father**.

Sara has wondered, what it would have been like to have her husband die rather than abuse and abandon her. Would it have

|  | **MEN** | **WOMEN** |
|---|---|---|
| Unfair stereotyping | If men cry, they are wimps. | If women get angry, they are bitches. |
| Confronting Problems | Usually stuff, and don't want to talk about it.<br><br>Want to move on or flee. | Usually want to talk it out. Sometimes to the point of irritation.<br><br>Grind right through the problem. |
| Processing Problems | Men process, then talk. | Women talk as they process. |

been worse? (We need to state that losing a spouse any way is hard, and that it depends on the individual circumstances. Many times death is worse than abuse/abandonment) Sara asked her friend Pearl, who had lost her husband of twenty-nine years to cancer, that particular question. Pearl said that Sara's situation was worse. Sara began to disagree with Pearl, because Sara didn't have to watch her husband battle cancer for four years. Pearl countered with, "*Oh, but yes, Sara, you had to deal with cancer too. This cancer that I am talking about was your husband's mistreatment and abandonment of you. This cancer attacked your self-concept and dignity. Sure we both grieved, but I didn't have to repair my self-concept and dignity like you did.*"

### 3. Self-abuse/Self-sabotage

This phenomenon is first and foremost when dealing with abuse. The irony is that most people don't realize their existence of self-abuse nor its effects. Self abuse is the inappropriate manner of mistreating oneself. Most abused people show their scars by making bad choices. It can be as obvious as abusing drugs, purposely hurting your body, habitually drinking too much alcohol. . . . It also can be as subtle as poor eating habits, not exercising, staying in an emotionally abusive situation, not finishing the tasks at hand. . . . Self-abuse is detrimental to each person's quality of life. It tears away at their own self-concept, rendering many people dysfunctional.

Most of us have had hard times in our lives, and for some perhaps even abuse. However, we don't need to pile more abuse or difficulties on ourselves! **We need to take care of ourselves, because there are no guarantees that someone else will to do it for us.** Besides, that special someone, who is "helping" us, could be abusing us at the same time.

It is amazing how many people do not think about taking care of themselves! Let's take an example of a student named Paul. Some teenagers have incredible tragedies that they have to endure. They need to make sure they are taking care of themselves. Therefore encouraging them to keep up on their studies is a good start. Sometimes they think that this is absurd considering their situation. When Paul was told, *"Okay, your dad is abusive and is trying to ruin your life. Why should you let his craziness dominate your whole life? What do you have control of? Your grades, right? Then why destroy this part of your life? Study, graduate, and get out of the house. Then you will be able to get on with your life!"*

Paul was relieved immediately, because he realized that in spite of it all, he did have some control over his destiny. Paul acknowledged that he had control over the friends he chooses, to eat right, to exercise, and to stay away from drugs and alcohol. In the past it never occurred to Paul that he should take care of himself, that he can control part of his life, and most importantly, that he had and will always have the *choice* to take that control.

### a. The Arrows of Choice

Note the following diagram, which depicts the quality of Paul's life. The optimum quality of life is ten points. This is when everything is going perfect. Note that zero represents the worst quality of life. In this level most everything is going tragically wrong. The big thick arrow shows how Paul's quality of life has been temporarily diminished due to various situations that are out of his control. Currently his quality of life has been lowered to the level four.

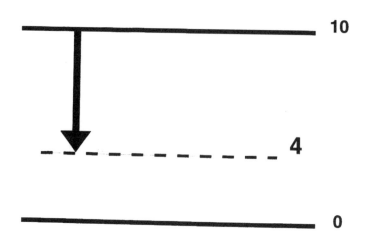

The next graphic shows how Paul can improve or ruin his quality of life. The thin lines represent what Paul does have under his control, such as: taking drugs or alcohol, school grades, eating, exercising, and choosing friends. Notice, every little bit helps or hurts. Paul's quality of life can be improved to the level 8 or ruined to the level 0.

One can see that Paul does have a lot of control over his life. Granted some of his situations have made his life worse, even to the level four. However, the control that Paul has is quite substantial. His choice and actions determine whether his quality of life can be as high as eight or as low as zero. This visual aid helps us all realize that various situations can have some control over our lives, but each one of us has some power to change our quality of life.

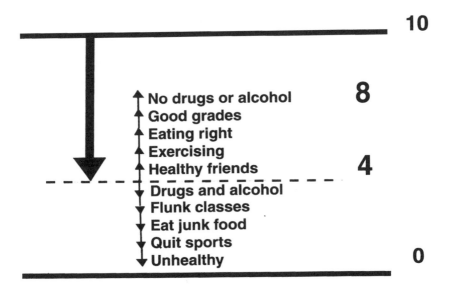

**10**

↑ **No drugs or alcohol**   **8**
↑ **Good grades**
↑ **Eating right**
↑ **Exercising**
↑ **Healthy friends**   **4**
↓ **Drugs and alcohol**
↓ **Flunk classes**
↓ **Eat junk food**
↓ **Quit sports**
↓ **Unhealthy**   **0**

**Remember pain may happen, but misery is your choice!!**

Now draw your own situation. Draw where your quality of life is due to other circumstances. Then draw where your quality of life could be if you start making good choices. Finally list those choices that you have under your control.

10

0

**What I can control:**
1.
2.
3.
4.
5.
6.

As adults, we often are no better at taking care of ourselves. The amount of self-abuse, whether conscious or subconscious, is alarmingly common. For instance, there are many spouses who ignore their partners and are oblivious to their needs. Many times the ignorer has the *benefits* of being married and single, while the ignored has the *frustrations* of being married and sin-

131

gle. The ignored partner becomes frustrated and starts to give up. They may become so depressed that they won't exercise, eat right, or stimulate themselves intellectually. They may wrap themselves up in television, booze, or become a social hermit. Yes, the ignored may not have control over everything, but they do have control in some areas of their life.

**There are enough people who make your life frustrating, but it is your choice whether you make it miserable or not!**

### b. Self-love vs. self-sabotage

Think of someone (or a couple of people) whom you deeply love and cherish your relationship with them. Now ask yourself the following questions:

1. Do you love them so much that you would always be there to help them?
2. Do you enjoy doing things for them to make their lives easier?
3. Isn't it true that you would never think of abusing, hurting, or mistreating them?

If you answered yes to the previous questions, then you know how to encourage, nurture, and improve the quality of life of other people. Now let's take a look at yourself. If you would never do any harm and always try to do good for your friends, then why wouldn't you do the same thing for yourself? We all need to work hard at self-love, so that we can take care of ourselves instead of destroying our lives. At times it is hard to love oneself, but this self-love is crucial.

### c. Subtle forms of self-abuse

A more subtle form of self-abuse is the ignorance, or defiance, to improving ones health in **all** areas of their life. For instance workaholics will stay busy so that they don't have to deal with anything else. Some religious people pursue their faith with fervor, but they are physically out of shape, emotionally depressed due to the denial of their other needs. Then there are the socialites who just party all the time, ruin their bodies with drugs and alcohol, continually spend their money like crazy, and have hard times holding down their jobs.

All self-abuse, whether subtle or not, needs to be confronted and removed!

## H. Misconception: Abused people are weak people!

It is amazing to see the amount of abuse that goes on daily. The numbers and statistics are just appalling. *"In fact the U.S. Surgeon General in 1992 ranked abuse by husbands and partners as the leading cause of injuries to women ages 15–44, causing them more harm than vehicular accidents, rapes, and muggings combined."*

It is often thought that abused people, especially women, are very weak people who couldn't make it on their own and preferred to remain abused rather than be alone. Yes, some abused people fit that description. However, many abused victims are very strong people:

1. They choose to stay in the relationship to try to rescue it. They made vows, *". . . for better and worse, until death do us part . . ."* and don't want to give up when the going gets rough.
2. They can't bear to watch their spouse, child, parent, friend destroying their own life. The abused feel that it is their duty to help the abuser bring their life around.
3. Most women have to deal with the cultural and traditional expectations. In many places the women are supposed to be the "peace maker" by ignoring their own feelings and needs in order that they can please their partner. This way there will always be peace in the relationship, but there will be a lot of sacrificed needs and later bitter feelings for the female.
4. Finally there is the pride/failure issue. For example, some people might say . . . *"If I divorce, or get out of my situation, then I am a failure. What will my parents, neighbors, church members, family, friends say?"*

133

One day Sara journaled, *"I am divorced, abused, abandoned, and clinically depressed. And it is OK! Definitely the bad treatment is not OK, but who I am is OK. I am no less loved or usable to society. In fact, I probably can help a lot of people out!"*

# I. Recovery from abuse.

Referring back to chapter 8 on self-affirmation, a special category has been added. It is when people are in the recovery phase from abuse. Whether it was self-inflicted, or from someone else, self-affirmation is the key.

**Recovery from abuse:**

1. I am making it "moment by moment."
2. Step by step, inch by inch, I am doing do it.
3. Just for today, I will be chemically free. (I.e., smoke free.)
4. I am fine on my own. I can do it.
5. Each day I feel better about myself.
6. Today I will encourage someone who has the same healing journey that I have.
7. I am healing! I will overcome!

*Personal notes and ideas*

What have I learned about abuse from this book?

What abuse have I actually experienced?

What have been some of my telltales/wake-up calls?

Who has withdrawn too much out of my relationship account?

How can I let my emotions out safely and effectively?

How have I been self-abusive?

What steps can I take to stop the abuse? (Whether self-inflicted or not.)

# 15

# Abandonment

## A. Definition

The majority of abandonment is due to the fact that the person is running from something. They are either running from responsibility, tragedy, or commitment. They believe that they can find a "better" life if they run away and start over. It is the old saying, *"The grass is greener on the other side of the hill."* Abandonment is when someone chooses to renege on a relationship commitment without considering the needs of the other person. Parents abandon children, spouses abandon their partners, children run out on their parents, friends turn their backs on other friends. . . .

Just as there are many forms of abuse, there are also various types of abandonment. Some people choose to leave abruptly without giving the other person a chance to do anything. This abandonment is like an unexpected death, such as a car accident, gun shot wound, or a sudden heart attack. There is little to no forewarning, and it comes as an absolute shock. Then there is the slow and painful abandonment, which is likened to a terminally ill death, such as cancer. There is a lot of emotional abandonment and abuse before the abandoner finally leaves. In addition, when one abandons another person, they are usually abandoning themselves too. This self-abandonment phenomenon results in the ignoring, and sometimes the destruction, of one's self-worth, dignity, and pride. Finally, there is the abandonment of suicide, which is devastating to all the loved ones. Usually the survivors have to deal with the guilt of not doing enough, saying the right thing, or being there for their depressed friend. These survivors need to be reassured that it was the other person's choice to end his/her life and shouldn't beat themselves up emotionally. The end result of any form of abandonment is pain, heartache, confusion, a shattered self-concept, and many times a refusal to trust again.

## B. Pain—the #1 cause of abandonment.

Most people wonder, *"Why do people leave others? What have I done to deserve this? How can people do something like this? I would never dream of doing anything this selfish...."* The reason for the majority of this abandonment phenomenon is that the abandoner is running from something that is causing them pain. When people have so much pain in their lives, and refuse to confront it, they usually choose to run from everything and everyone. They even run from themselves! Abandoners usually shut down all of their common sense, dignity, emotions, and just run.

Life can be tough, and we all will need to deal with pain sooner or later. If we choose to love and cherish others, we run the risk of getting our hearts broken.

Where there was love, there is grief.

—Anonymous

If there is love, and it is gone, there will be heartache. Pain is real, it is there, and we can't hide from it. **WE DEFINITELY SHOULD NOT RUN FROM IT!** Avoiding pain can lead to abandonment, which can emotionally paralyze and destroy someone. Moreover, ignored pain not only aids in the self-destruction of the **person in denial**, but also destroys the lives of the **closest and dearest people** to that person. Instead of facing the truth, the abandoner chooses the easy way out running from all their problems. They aren't necessarily running from *the person they love*, but running from their *past*. It is too scary for them to face their past, because it is like walking into a house that is on fire. Therefore they will do whatever it takes to avoid entering into that pain.

Let's face it, there are troubles everywhere. Robbery, rape, weather storms, violence, sickness, loss of job, accidents . . . happen all over the world. You are not immune to pain anywhere in this world. So why run? Over the long haul, running is more damaging and a lot more work. If you choose to run away from your pain and never face your problems, a vicious circle of abandonment can begin. The following circle shows that if you are running from tragedy, you are not only abandoning your loved ones, but your own self too.

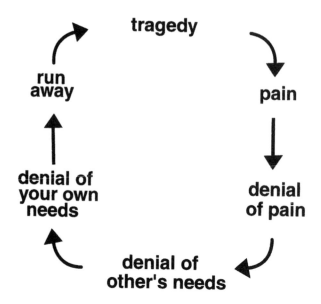

The consequence of abandonment is that people can get overwhelmed with all of the problems that they have ignored. Meanwhile, the pile of problems gets bigger and bigger. This happens for two reasons. The first is that more problems are being added to the pile. The second is that the problems that are already there, grow like interest for loans. The longer the person ignores their pain, the more guilt, frustration, depression, and anger will grow to paralyzing terms so that they can no longer function responsibly. They feel so out of control that they just give up on everything and stuff their pain as far away as possible. Thus, they continue to retreat, run, hide, lie, deny, and ruin their lives.

> The past is a choice!
> You can either <u>run</u> from it,
> or you can <u>learn</u> from it.
>
> —The Author

Pain and heartache travel real well. If you choose to run, they will run right along with you. It is best to face the truth, because it doesn't go away no matter how fast or far you run. It keeps coming after you until you turn around and face it. Someday, somehow you will need to come back home and face your situation. Therefore, the sooner the better for everyone involved.

## C. Misconceptions

### 1. I would never do it so therefore it is difficult for people to do . . . UNFORTUNATELY IT IS EASY TO DO!

It's amazing how easy it is for people to get up and walk out. They completely shut down by medicating themselves with the ever-so-popular, DENIAL. Somehow their consciences get turned off, and they make little to no sense at all. People who abandon others just don't get it and have many reasons (excuses) for their actions.

### 2. The people nearest and dearest to me would never do this . . . BUT IT CAN BE THE LEAST PERSON YOU WOULD EXPECT!

Not only does abandonment happen from mere acquaintances, but from <u>WHOM</u> you least expect. The closest people in your life can turn away from you at any time. It's unfathomable! Believe it or not, while Sara was processing her abandonment from her husband, one of Sara's dearest friends chose to move on with her life. This was very hard to take because they still lived in the same town. Sara had little to no say in the matter, nor had she done anything to deserve her friend's selfish actions. To be honest, this perplexed Sara more than her own husband's desertion. You just never know!!!

139

**3. Abandonment doesn't happen often, because most people are faithful. BUT IT'S SO COMMON!**

Unfortunately abandonment is common and the frequency of this phenomenon is devastating. Some people are making various terrible decisions these days. For example, they are choosing to be sexual when they are still very immature. They try to raise the child, and when the going gets tough, they run. They are only thinking of themselves. Their selfish actions are scarring this child for life! Abandonment has a traumatic effect on people, which can render them emotionally disabled for some time. We have all been given the ability to conquer the pain of abandonment and move on with our lives. However, it takes a lot of commitment, energy, time, courage, and faith to overcome this inhumane treatment.

In this day and age, some people are not taking responsibility for their actions. Take responsibility for your actions, especially if it involves another person. Don't try to take the easy way out, because it is too hurtful to others.

**4. Abandonment is only physical . . . NOT NECESSARILY SO!**

Most people think that abandonment is when people leave the house and never come back. Abandonment isn't just a physical phenomenon, but it is an emotional one too. Even thought the person is still living with you, they could be abandoning you emotionally. Most of the time, they will busy themselves with other tasks and choose not to deal with the problem.

For example, Scott was living in the same house with his wife, but she was emotionally out of the relationship for some time. She didn't let him know what was on her mind and chose to relieve her frustrations through other activities. During this time she was hoping that her emotional tie would rejuvenate again. By not addressing the situation, she shut down emotionally and blamed Scott for not meeting her emotional needs. Then before Scott knew it, she was out the door. This is typical in most situations like Scott's, the "emotional" abandoners usually don't give the spouse the chance to repair the relationship and just walk. Abandonment doesn't necessarily begin when the person physically walks out of your life, but it can happen emotionally much earlier.

Emotional abandonment, whether conscious or subconscious, is a form of abuse. It is at this point where abuse and abandonment overlap. When someone abandons a relationship emotionally, they are abusing that other person by ignoring them and showing indifference. Refer to the following diagram. Notice that the two circles of abandonment and abuse overlap, because situations like Scott's can be labeled either way.

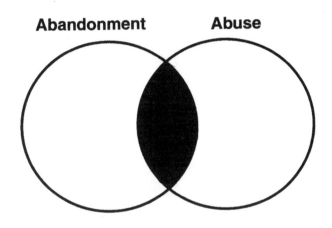

**Abandonment**        **Abuse**

### 5. Spouses don't leave each other when the going gets tough. THIS IS TRUE SOMETIMES, BUT MANY TIMES IT IS NOT.

Being abandoned is never convenient, but it could come at the absolute worst time of your life. Unfortunately, tragedy does funny things to people. It either makes or breaks the relationship. Everyone grieves differently, and unfortunately some choose to shut down. They shut down on themselves, close friends, and sometimes even their faith. It is really hard on the other spouse who is trying to weather the tragedy. They are doing whatever possible to stay afloat, while the other one is just giving up on everything.

You can probably guess what happens next. Yes, the quitter leaves the courageous person who is battling the problem. This is an harsh slap in the face to the person who is trying to survive the tragedy. Now they have to deal with their tragedy and the awful fact of being abandoned.

**6. If I am abandoned, then I am obviously not worth much ... YOU ARE A WORTHWHILE PERSON AND CAN BE A CONTRIBUTING CITIZEN.**

Abandonment happens in all forms, and it also happens to all types of people. Whether you are rich, poor, educated, blue collar, white collar professional, no one is immune to abandonment. Many times the abandoner has no reason to leave, nor has the other person given them a reason to leave. Most abandoned people become frustrated because their break-up was not a "we" decision, but a selfish "me" decision. The pain is amazing. However, **WE ARE NO LESS OF A PERSON IF WE ARE UNDERGOING PAIN!** Some say that in order to be a contributing citizen of this world, you have to have it all together. On the contrary, many people have found in their weakest times that they have been able to make a positive impact in other people's lives. The unfortunate falsehood that a grieving person is not only ineffective, much less a burden to society, has unjustly permeated society.

## D. Reactions

### 1. You feel like trash

When someone is abandoned, without a choice in the matter, *they feel like trash*. Their age, financial status, occupation, gender, or what kind of self-concept they had prior to the abandonment doesn't matter. Each abandoned person feels lower than low, because their self-concept has been totally shattered. One may deny it for a while and say that they are just fine, but that is a major cover-up. Being abandoned is one of the worst, if not the most devastating, feelings that anyone could ever experience. One abandoned wife said to a widow. *"You don't know what it is like. If you are a widow, you are respected by the people. How-*

*ever if your husband has left you, there is no respect. Everyone is wondering what you did wrong."* This is what Sara wrote in her journal upon accepting the truth of her situation. *"Now it is all coming to me. I am finally digesting that I am an ABANDONED wife, friend, girlfriend . . . OUCH! I was abandoned! Damn!"*

## 2. Anger and Abandonment

Many people will refrain from anger because they feel that it is inappropriate. They have been taught to be tolerant, patient, understanding. . . . However, there should be no tolerance, patience, or understanding for people who choose to walk out and destroy another person's life. In these situations, anger is not only appropriate but necessary! There are both healthy and inappropriate bursts of rage. The lesson to be learned is that anger is a feeling that can't be ignored, but it needs to be dealt with properly. Refer to Pages 38 and 39 in the first part of the book.

## 3. Grief and abandonment

Sara grieved the loss of her husband and thought that she had it all together. Then one year later, Sara found that she had to deal with the abandonment issue. It hit her like a lead brick. It wasn't just the abandonment of her husband, but of all the other people who chose to run out on her. To Sara's amazement she actually took the abandonment issue harder than when she lost her husband. The pain of his leaving, lies, false promises was very painful. However actually accepting the whole abandonment phenomenon was devastating. This really surprised Sara, because she thought that each layer should get easier. That is not necessarily the case. Some layers are easier than others. Some take very little energy out of you, while others will totally debilitate you.

Also in processing pain from abandonment, don't look at the whole picture and try to conquer it. With abandonment being so unfathomable, it is too much for us to handle all at once. The situation has left us as walking time bombs, therefore we need to tackle it piece by piece so that we don't explode.

> There is no right way to grieve. There is just <u>YOUR</u> way."
>
> —Rusty Berkus

## E. Enough is enough! Learn to say "NO."

Unfortunately some of your friends need to leave for good reasons. Then there are the friends who just selfishly take off and leave you in the dust. We tend to ask ourselves, *"What have I done to deserve this?"* Nine time out of ten, we have done absolutely nothing to deserve this terrible mistreatment! You will need to work overtime to make sure that your self-concept is not destroyed. You will *continually* need to reassure yourself that the other person's actions were selfish and inappropriate. They may be struggling, very wrapped up in themselves, or just plain incoherent to the situation. No matter what the reason is, their abandonment hurts and was wrong!

Learn to say "NO" to these self-centered "friends," and put an end to destructive relationships. Our response to this inhumane treatment, should be the same. **Don't put up with it!** There is a point in time where we have to say "**BASTA**." That means "enough" in Spanish. We need to assertively tell the other people that what they are doing is not OK If they don't listen, and they probably won't, that is *their* problem. However, we need to firmly speak our peace, without being abusive or vengeful, for our own dignity.

## F. Healing/Moving On

### 1. It doesn't make sense.

If you are having a hard time trying to make sense out of your abandonment, don't be dismayed. Abandonment and abuse don't make any sense at all! There may be times when you need to change your focus from trying to understand your mistreatment to moving on with your life. All that happened to you goes against everything you believe in emotionally and morally. The core of your being may be to stand by your loved ones through thick and thin. You may never understand the abandonment phenomenon. Therefore, in order to move on with your life, you may have to just accept that it happened. Don't allow someone else's selfish actions to make you become emotionally paralyzed. So get angry, grieve, process the hurt, forgive, and go on with your life. **Many times we need not focus on how to *get over it*, but on how to *go on* with it!**

## 2. Healing activities for grief

There are many avenues for people to grieve and heal in a positive manner. The point is not to busy yourself so that you become incoherent to your pain. These activities are to help you channel your grief into a positive outcome so that you can fully heal. The following are plans of action to help you overcome your grief:

1. Plant a tree in memory of the person who just died.
2. Start a new crusade. (M.A.D.D., fund-raising efforts for the African-American churches that have been burnt to the ground, AIDS awareness, etc. . . .)
3. Set up a scholarship in memory of the person or event.
4. Sing a song in their honor.
5. Set up a fund-raising event for your certain cause.
6. Volunteer your time to your particular cause.
7. Artistic expression—Paint, do ceramics, dance . . .
8. Have a huge media release to educate people of the dangers.
9. Write a book.
10. Write to your congressman.
11. Redecorate various rooms with new wall art. **(Please add your ideas)**
12.
13.
14.

And the list goes on. . . . Yes, we can make lemonade out of lemons if we have the right attitude and choose to do so.

## G. The waving arm. It is tough to trust again.

People who have been abandoned really have a tough time when it comes to trusting again. They will definitely need some extra tender loving care (TLC). As much as they try to forget and go on with their lives, those ugly memories surface every now and then. Most of them are triggered by a something familiar to their abandonment. Whether it be smelling the same cologne, hearing certain words, listening to a song from the past, witnessing a similar situation . . . usually they shut down because the old memories and feelings come back in a flash and are as strong as ever.

Remember the story of the *Man of the House* on page 31. At the beginning of the movie, a man walks out on his wife and child. The child has a very vivid memory of the father driving away with his arm out of the window waving good-bye. Later in the movie, he saw a stranger driving away and waving out the window. He immediately reverted back to the time when his father left him. He was overcome with sadness. Another time his mother's new boyfriend was taking her out to dinner. As they drove away, the boyfriend waved out the window. This threw the young boy into despair and refusal to trust this man.

Everyone who has been abandoned will have to deal with memories like the "waving arm." Just be prepared, know that they will come, that it is natural, and that they can be overcome. It is so important that we verbalize this fear of abandonment and the "waving arm" to our loved ones and newly found friends. It can be hard for people who have not been abandoned to understand why the other one shuts down. Although they may not be able to *empathize* with us, hopefully they can *sympathize* and try their best to be patient with us. What we need the most is PATIENCE and UNDERSTANDING.

One day Sara journaled about trusting other people. *"It's so hard. After such continual pain. I want to trust, I know I should. I* *guess that I'm in too much in pain, but what I am learning is that this is where trust begins. When we are so out of it and don't want to go on. When we make the **choice** to go on, is also when we start trusting."*

Trusting is a process, just as life and healing are. But every process needs to be started, and that is where our choice comes in to play. Unfortunately, many times we have to choose to start that process of trusting when we are emotionally drained.

## H. According to C.S. Lewis

The loss of a loved one is one of the most painful things that anyone could ever experience. Whether it is a sudden death, a slow relentless dying process, abandonment . . . it is tough! After being abandoned most people have a hard time loving another person, because they are so afraid of being abandoned again. It is similar with people who have lost loved ones due to death. They do not want to open themselves up to another person, because they are afraid that the new significant other will die. However, in abandonment, there is a choice, and it is very tough to accept the fact that someone **chose** to leave you. Therefore we put up walls! *"If I don't let someone in, then I don't have to deal with the pain later when I lose them."*

C. S. Lewis put it so well: **TO RISK BEING HURT IS TO BE VULNERABLE**:

To love at all is to be vulnerable. Love anything, and your heart will certainly be wrung and possibly be broken. If you want to make sure of keeping it intact, you must give your heart to no one, not even to an animal. Wrap it round with hobbies and little luxuries; avoid all entanglements; lock it up safe in the casket or coffin of your selfishness. But in that casket—safe, dark, motionless, airless—it will change. It will not be broken; it will become unbreakable, impenetrable, irredeemable. The alternative to tragedy, or at least the risk of tragedy, is damnation. The only place outside Heaven where you can be perfectly safe from all the dangers and perturbations of love is Hell.

147

*Personal notes and ideas*

How did I feel after being abandoned?

What kind of emotions did I experience?

What was the worst part of my abandonment?

What is my "waving arm"? What triggers my pain from past abandonments?

How can I heal so that these waving arms don't have such a huge effect on me?

What activity can I do to help me heal and also be of benefit to others?